IMAGES
of America

ANGLICANS IN NORTH JERSEY

THE EPISCOPAL DIOCESE OF NEWARK

On the cover: Scores of Sunday school children gathered outside Grace Episcopal Church in Nutley on October 11, 1925, in this small piece of a much larger portrait, another portion of which appears inside. It was taken during the tenure of Rev. Charles P. Tinker, a graduate of Boston University, class of 1892. (Courtesy of Grace Episcopal Church, Nutley.)

IMAGES
of America

ANGLICANS IN NORTH JERSEY

THE EPISCOPAL DIOCESE OF NEWARK

Philip M. Read
Foreword by
Rt. Rev. John Palmer Croneberger

ARCADIA
PUBLISHING

ISBN 978-0-7385-6267-4

Published by Arcadia Publishing
Charleston SC, Chicago IL, Portsmouth NH, San Francisco CA

Printed in the United States of America

Library of Congress Catalog Card Number: 2008933016

For all general information contact Arcadia Publishing at:
Telephone 843-853-2070
Fax 843-853-0044
E-mail sales@arcadiapublishing.com
For customer service and orders:
Toll-Free 1-888-313-2665

Visit us on the Internet at www.arcadiapublishing.com

William Marsden Read Jr. was born in Paterson in 1898, the first of six children of immigrants from Macclesfield, England, who came to work in the bustling mills of America's "Silk City." By 1923, he was living in Rochelle Park and hurried off with Stephanie D. Thompson of Maywood to "the Little Church around the Corner" in New York City to wed on April 14, 1923. The excursion to the big city was not unusual. In ensuing years, their oldest son, William M. Read III, would be darting across Maywood's Oak Avenue to don his altar boy vestments at St. Martin's Episcopal Church. In Newark, the label "the Little Church around the Corner" was used to describe Trinity Church in a 1906 article in the *Newark Daily Advertiser.*

Contents

Acknowledgments

There are certain people who made this pictorial work possible. As such, words of thanks go to Rt. Rev. John Palmer Croneberger, ninth bishop of Newark, for contributing the foreword; Michael Francaviglia, diocesan administrator, for his ongoing assistance; and Cecil Broner, sexton of Episcopal House, for his help in accessing the diocesan archives. Unless otherwise noted, images appear courtesy of the author.

As an apology from an Episcopal author, this was taken from the 25th anniversary booklet of 1939, St. Bartholomew's Church, Ho-Ho-Kus, New Jersey:

> Your historiographers beg your indulgent sympathy in the reading of this paper. They know that there are many inaccuracies in it and that they have slighted, and in cases completely overlooked, aspects of the work dear to many members of the parish. They have, as was inevitable, emphasized those projects in which they have had a part or have been most interested. In excuse they plead the shortness of the time allotted . . . and the well-known prejudices of the human mind.

FOREWORD

It was 1980, after 17 years in the Diocese of Bethlehem, when my bishop, Lloyd Gressle, reminded me that the church was larger than any one diocese, and perhaps I should be open to the larger church. It did not take long. I had the opportunity to meet Bishop Jack Spong at the General Convention in 1979. He was recruiting clergy for the Diocese of Newark, and my name was added to the list. By the fall of 1980, we had moved to Tenafly, New Jersey, and I became a new priest in the Diocese of Newark. Twenty-six years later, I resigned as bishop of Newark, to begin a period of retirement.

During those 26 years, I had the privilege of serving in a diocese that seemed to be filled with people eager to explore the issues of our time within the context of a faith community. A series of task forces were created during that time, each exploring at some depth a particular issue. Discussion and debate filled the air. Sometimes we were able to bring some light to the matter at hand; sometimes we brought more heat than light to the table; and sometimes I am certain we brought neither heat nor light.

To this day, the Diocese of Newark continues to engage the issues of our time, seeking to stir both minds and passions into some appropriate action or response. In so doing, we frequently find ourselves face to face with the risen Christ who bids us to come.

If you have not had the opportunity to experience life within an Episcopal community of faith, I bid you to come to the water—you will always be welcome.

—Rt. Rev. John Palmer Croneberger
Ninth Bishop of Newark

INTRODUCTION

Who has not taken the journey with Judy Garland as Dorothy as she makes her way down the yellow brick road in *The Wizard of Oz*? Or the trek with Moses to the top of Mount Sinai in Cecil B. DeMille's *The Ten Commandments*? The Christian seasons are all about journeys—not unlike those of Dorothy and Moses.

But what some might not know is actress Judy Garland and director Cecil B. DeMille were also Episcopalians. They were in good company. So too were George Washington, the nation's first president; Betsy Ross, the famed flag maker; Natalie Cole, daughter of Nat "King" Cole; and Buzz Aldrin, who stepped on the moon right after Neil Armstrong in that historic lunar walk in 1969.

At one point or another, many Americans have walked through the traditionally massive red doors of a parish that is part of the Protestant Episcopal Church of America, itself a part of the larger worldwide Anglican Communion that has its roots in England.

Perhaps nowhere is the history of this storied religious institution more evident than in the Episcopal Diocese of Newark, which can trace its beginnings to 1729. It was a movement built on the shoulders of early missionaries, among them John Talbot, the "Apostle of New Jersey."

It was never an easy struggle. With the American Revolution, the clergy, who had sworn allegiance to the British Crown, were assaulted and imprisoned. When the revolutionary zeal had ended, there remained only 20 ailing congregations considered "baggage left behind" by the monarch.

The diocese's first bishop, John Croes, was not consecrated until 1815. Yet he came with a different set of credentials, having served in the Continental army during the American Revolution.

In the years to come, growth was such that by 1874, there were 64 parishes and the need to create a diocese for the northern seven counties distinct from the rest of New Jersey. In 1886, the name Diocese of Newark was born.

By the century's close, parishes were born, some struggling to work God's mission on Earth. In Clifton, one fledging mission, St. Peter's, was greeted this way by the press. "There are too few Episcopalians in Clifton to succeed," a newspaper writer proclaimed. "The few trying to start a church there are placing upon their shoulders a burden that will be an oppression to then for the next 20 years." The prediction proved to be flawed. In 2008, the parish, which has ridden the boom and bust cycle of postwar Protestantism, was marking its 112th year, administering to spiritual seekers of Jesus Christ.

Its faithful story is but one of many in a diocese with 114 parishes spread out over northern New Jersey, representing a great suburban ring outside New York City, in the most densely populated state in the nation.

One

Newark and the Oranges

Lift high the cross, the love of Christ proclaim
Till all the world adore his sacred Name.

—"Lift High the Cross," No. 473, *The Hymnal* 1982

The tower of Trinity Cathedral reaches skyward above the trees of Newark's Military Park in this mid-20th-century postcard scene. The c. 1809 church retains the original tower of the 1744 house of worship, making it the oldest piece of masonry in the city. According to a 1970 *Newark News* article, it is Newark's second-oldest congregation, formed in 1732 by sympathizers of Col. Josiah Ogden, a member of Newark's first church, Old First, who is said to have left after being censured for harvesting his wheat crop on a Sunday.

In 1966, Trinity Cathedral and St. Philip's Church merged into the historic Broad Street church, bringing together a white and black congregation in a diocese soon to be at the forefront of social change. The next year, when urban rioting erupted in America's cities, Trinity and St. Philip's Cathedral sponsored the first national conference on black empowerment, the Inner City Urban Leadership Conference. By 1969, the Canon Dillard Robinson became dean of the cathedral, the first African American to serve in that capacity in any Episcopal cathedral in the nation. Bishop Leland Stark, an early supporter of the ordination of women, was also active in the peace movement during the Vietnam War and served as a cochair of Negotiation Now. (Courtesy of the Episcopal Diocese of Newark.)

Rt. Rev. Thomas Alfred Starkey, who hailed from St. Paul's Episcopal Church, Paterson, was elected bishop on October 28, 1879, and consecrated the following January 8. It was under Starkey that the then Diocese of Northern Jersey became the Diocese of Newark after a series of actions culminating in 1887. (Courtesy of the Episcopal Diocese of Newark.)

Newark's Grace Episcopal Church, the city's second Episcopal church, was founded in 1837 by prominent Newark families. By 1854, the congregation had built today's Grace Episcopal Church atop the foundation of the old Essex County Jail. In 1910, Rev. Elliot White, left, served as rector at a time when Newark had 16 Episcopal parishes. Reverend White is credited with creating the first choir camp, according to Leonard Ellinwood's *History of American Church Music*. Among Grace Episcopal Church's notable parishioners was William Stryker Gummere, who was chief justice of the New Jersey Supreme Court. In 1932, his funeral was held at the Gothic church at Broad and Walnut Streets. Years later, Grace Episcopal Church's connection to the old courthouse made for some good copy in the *Newark Evening News*. "The cells are still there but walled off," reporter Howard R. Garis wrote. "And the reason for the walling shut is that mischievous choir boys, at practice in the church, often locked neophytes in them." (Courtesy of the Episcopal Diocese of Newark.)

St. Barnabas in Newark is said to owe its inception to a layman by the name of William Dusenbury, with the first service being on September 12, 1852. A *c.* 1855 frame church was destroyed by fire in 1862, leading to the building of a stone one, above, on St. Barnabas Day, 1864. Among the later events at the church, at Warren Street and Sussex Avenue, was the awarding of a Cross of the Royal Order of King George I to its rector, Rev. Harry V. B. Darlington, the son of Bishop James H. Darlington of Harrisburg, Pennsylvania. In 1920, when Harry Darlington served at St. Barnabas, there were 17 Episcopal churches in Newark alone. (Courtesy of the Episcopal Diocese of Newark.)

The Wardens and Vestry of

ST. BARNABAS CHURCH

Warren St. and Sussex Ave., Newark, N. J.

request your attendance at service

Sunday Evening, December 19th, at 7:45 o'clock

when their rector

Rev. HARRY V. B. DARLINGTON

will be invested with

the Cross of the Royal Order of King George I

conferred on him by the Greek Goverment

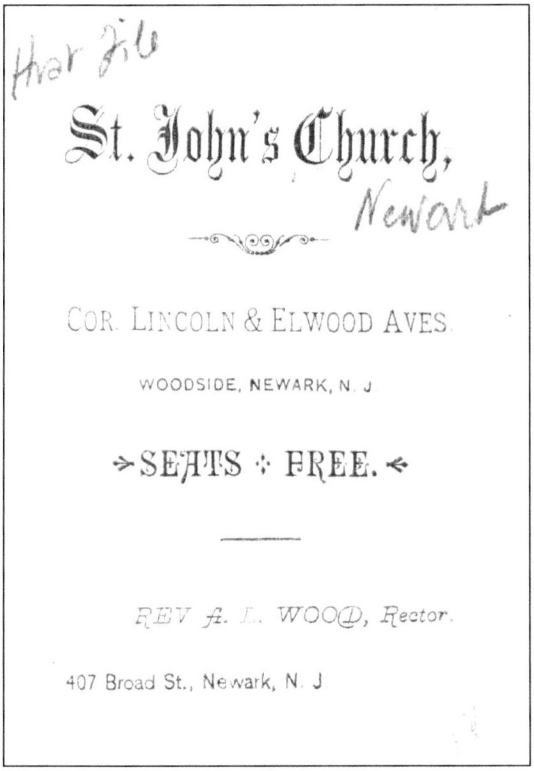

St. John's Church,
Newark

COR. LINCOLN & ELWOOD AVES.

WOODSIDE, NEWARK, N. J.

SEATS FREE.

REV A. L. WOOD, Rector.

407 Broad St., Newark, N. J.

"Seats Free" reads the booklet from St. John's Church at Lincoln and Elwood Avenues in Newark, where Rev. J. Frederic Hamblin presided over the congregation at its 65th anniversary in 1932. "St. John's is the oldest congregation in the north end of the city," reads a newspaper account, "Its first service was held Sept. 2, 1867." The 65th celebration came in Reverend Hamblin's 14th year as rector. It was a busy tenure with 129 baptisms, 105 confirmations, 75 weddings, and 169 funerals. (Courtesy of the Episcopal Diocese of Newark.)

St. Philip's Church, an African American congregation in Newark, was founded in 1848 in a schoolhouse on the southeast corner of Halsey and New Streets before building a brick house of worship on High Street near New Street. For many years before its founding, the parishioners were communicants at Trinity Cathedral, described as "the only parish in the city that has ever given it any large consideration." (Courtesy of the Episcopal Diocese of Newark.)

The little bulletin of Newark's St. Andrew's Episcopal Church in 1915 measured just three by five inches and carried such news as an update on the organ fund, with $638.20 that had been gathered to date. The church, at 871 South Seventeenth Street, was then led by Rev. Charles Henry Wells. (Courtesy of the Episcopal Diocese of Newark.)

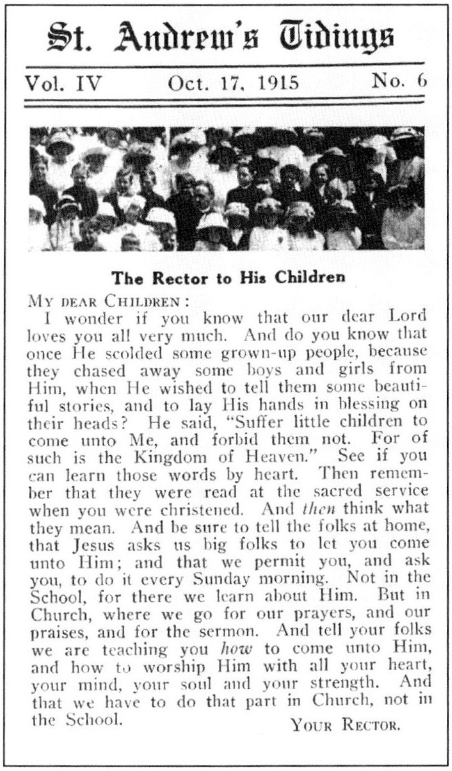

St. Andrew's Tidings

Vol. IV   Oct. 17, 1915   No. 6

The Rector to His Children

MY DEAR CHILDREN:

I wonder if you know that our dear Lord loves you all very much. And do you know that once He scolded some grown-up people, because they chased away some boys and girls from Him, when He wished to tell them some beautiful stories, and to lay His hands in blessing on their heads? He said, "Suffer little children to come unto Me, and forbid them not. For of such is the Kingdom of Heaven." See if you can learn those words by heart. Then remember that they were read at the sacred service when you were christened. And *then* think what they mean. And be sure to tell the folks at home, that Jesus asks us big folks to let you come unto Him; and that we permit you, and ask you, to do it every Sunday morning. Not in the School, for there we learn about Him. But in Church, where we go for our prayers, and our praises, and for the sermon. And tell your folks we are teaching you *how* to come unto Him, and how to worship Him with all your heart, your mind, your soul and your strength. And that we have to do that part in Church, not in the School.

YOUR RECTOR.

The Church of St. Mary Magdalene, at Newark's Pomona Avenue and North Parkview Terrace, was founded on October 12, 1913 and was thriving by its 25th anniversary in 1938. A vested girls' choir was forming. The boys' basketball team was undefeated. There were 11 new pledges counted. Sunday school enrollment hit 95, with average attendance in the 70s. "To everyone who reads this little folder, we say: Do not you want to share in this happy and life-giving work . . . Would you not like to stand with us?" wrote Karl G. Kumm, rector, and Merle Darling, for the vestry. (Courtesy of the Episcopal Diocese of Newark.)

The architectural firm of John H. and Wilson C. Ely had already made a name for itself when it designed the Diocesan House on Newark's Rector Street. On October 8, 1939, newspapers reported the plans for the building of English architecture to house offices that had been at 99 Main Street in Orange since 1929. The architectural firm in 1906 had already created Newark's elegant Beaux-Arts city hall and later, in 1931, the 34-story National Newark Building, whose top was modeled after the mausoleum at Halicarnassus, one of the seven wonders of the world, and remained New Jersey's tallest building until 1989. Here the Diocesan House and its All Saints Chapel are shown in 1941. (Courtesy of the Episcopal Diocese of Newark.)

In the then new Diocesan House, secretaries are settled into their new home. They are Jeanette DeHart (left), secretary to Rev. W. O. Leslie Jr., canon missioner, and Pauline Weber, secretary to Rev. A. S. Hogenauer, field secretary of the board of religious education. (Courtesy of the Episcopal Diocese of Newark.)

The Diocesan House came equipped with a library with built-in bookcases. Visitors in 1941 included (standing) Herbert Eason and Charlotte Birch. Those sitting are identified as, from left to right, May V. Frowappell, Albert Faux, Virginia J. Grabyne, and Doris K. Lawrence. (Courtesy of the Episcopal Diocese of Newark.)

Newark's House of Prayer was consecrated on November 26, 1850, with seating for 400 and, according to a 1908 history, became the first in the diocese to use lights, incense, and vestments. (Courtesy of the Episcopal Diocese of Newark.)

Episcopalian Bishop's Consecration Tuesday

6-3-53

Rev. Dr. Leland W. F. Stark Will Become Coadjutor of Newark Diocese at Trinity Cathedral

The first consecration of a bishop ever to take place within 210-year-old Trinity Cathedral will be held Tuesday at 10:30 A. M. when Rev. Dr. Leland William Frederick Stark becomes bishop coadjutor of the Episcopal Diocese of Newark.

Dr. Stark, who has been rector of the Church of the Epiphany in downtown Washington since 1948, will as bishop coadjutor serve as assistant to Bishop Benjamin M. Washburn with the right of succession on Bishop Washburn's retirement. The diocese embraces the seven northernmost counties in New Jersey. It has a clergy of 180 and more than 86,000 lay members.

The historic cathedral, originally a mission of the Church of England, has been renovated and redecorated recently.

250 Clergy to Take Part

More than 250 clergy and other Episcopal dignitaries will participate in the service, after forming a colorful procession to the cathedral from Cathedral House in Rector street in the robes of their offices. Two crucifers, Donald Rossnagle of the cathedral and Charles Williams of the

Other Participants

Rev. Alexander M. Rodger of Ridgewood will be master of ceremonies and Rev. Dr. George M. Plaskett, for 45 years rector of the Church of the Epihany in Orange, will be chaplain to the presiding bishop. Marshalls for the procession will be Rev. Albert O. Judd of Maplewood, Canon William O. Leslie Jr., archdeacon of Newark, and Ven. Sydney E. Grant of Arlington, archdeacon of Hudson.

Dr. Clark will be escorted to his place at the Communion rail by his attending presbyters, Rev. Warren E. Mace, his assistant at Epiphany, and Rev. Cornelius P. Trowbridge of Morristown.

Bishop Horace W. B. Donegan of New York will read the Epistle of Consecration from the Acts of the Apostles. Gospel verses will be read by Suffragan Bishop Theodore R. Ludlow of this diocese, who will retire July 14, his 70th birthday.

Sermon By Canon Wedel

After the recitation of the

Rev. Dr. Leland William Frederick Stark became coadjutor at the 210-year-old Trinity Cathedral, the first bishop to ever be consecrated there, according to a 1953 newspaper account, right. The event, too, was broadcast over WATV-Channel 13 in the early era of television. Stark went on to serve as bishop from 1958 to 1973, an event capped by his retirement dinner. (Courtesy of the Episcopal Diocese of Newark.)

The Essex House in Newark on April 10, 1956, was the crowded locale for dinner at an event for the Episcopal Advance Fund. That same month, a special convention for the Episcopal Advance Fund filled Newark's Trinity Cathedral. (Courtesy of the Episcopal Diocese of Newark.)

By the 1950s, the past came alive at Trinity Cathedral, Newark, with a visit from one of the descendants of the founders, identified only as Mr. Ogden, center, flanked by Bishop Benjamin M. Washburn and Dean Coburn. A priest by the same name, Rev. Uzal Ogden, served Trinity Cathedral as rector from 1788 until 1805. (Courtesy of the Episcopal Diocese of Newark.)

The official publication of the diocese was the *Newark Churchman*, whose February 1963 issue focused on the "revolutionary impact of urbanization" and how it threatened to divide the country into two cultures—one rich and one poor. Among the examples cited for dealing with the issue head-on was the work of Rev. Eugene Avery, vicar of St. Aidan's in Paterson, where a summer program was one of many initiated for young people. (Courtesy of the Episcopal Diocese of Newark.)

Rt. Rev. John Shelby Spong, the eighth bishop of Newark, was consecrated bishop on June 12, 1976. By his address at the 125th convention of the Diocese of Newark in January 1999, he was summing up a long career. "My hope is that in my professional life I will be best remembered as one who wrestled publicly with our faith, trying to free it from the shackles of the past so that it could live into the future," he said. "My last book, 'Why Christianity Must Change or Die,' is the summation of that theological struggle." Here he waves, left, in an undated photograph. (Courtesy of the Episcopal Diocese of Newark.)

As was the custom, head coverings were the order of the day in September 1955 as the General Convention of the Episcopal Church gathered in Honolulu. (Courtesy of the Episcopal Diocese of Newark.)

The 69th General Convention of the Episcopal Church, convening in Detroit in 1988, gave rise to the Episcopal Network for Economic Justice, as well as resolutions on such things as environmental stewardship. Other topics, too, were making headlines. Just a few months off the presses was Bishop John Shelby Spong's latest book, *Living in Sin?: A Bishop Rethinks Human Sexuality*. (Courtesy of the Episcopal Diocese of Newark.)

Bishop John Shelby Spong, shown in a photograph dated March 23, 1980, is the most published member of the House of Bishops of the Episcopal Church in the United States. His 20-plus books include 1992's *Rescuing the Bible from Fundamentalism: A Bishop Rethinks the Meaning of Scripture* and 2008's *Jesus for the Non-Religious*. His books have sold more than one million copies and been translated into most of the major languages of the world. (Courtesy of the Episcopal Diocese of Newark, photograph by Theodore Herrmann of Englewood.)

Bishop Edwin S. Lines laid the cornerstone for the Church of the Incarnation in East Orange on June 28, 1924, during the tenure of Rev. Carolus R. Webb, who first came to the Church of the Incarnation in 1914. "The communicants now number 301," the author of a brief early history wrote on a manual typewriter. "Bishop Lines would return on Feb. 8, 1925, to actually dedicate the church, whose architect was Josiah T. Tubby." (Courtesy of the Episcopal Diocese of Newark.)

Rev. Charles L. Pardee, in 1896, found himself as an early rector of St. Andrew's Episcopal Church in South Orange. Just four years before, a body of gentlemen called the "Syndicate" offered a piece of land on Center Street and Sterling Avenue for the erection of a church, which formally opened on July 2, 1893. During Pardee's rectorship, a parish house was opened in October 1900. The new parish was said to have been the handiwork of a chapter of the Brotherhood of St. Andrew at Grace Episcopal Church in Orange. (Courtesy of the Episcopal Diocese of Newark.)

The chapel was small, measuring just 20 by 30 feet, sitting on a 100-by-200-foot lot at Rhode Island Avenue and Amherst Street in East Orange's Elmwood section. The cornerstone of Chapel of the Ascension was laid by Rev. G. M. Plaskett as work began on what was deemed "a fine piece of missionary endeavor." That ceremony came on July 30, 1922, the seventh Sunday after Trinity, in the presence of the congregants of the Church of the Epiphany in Orange. "The chapel, of course, is an extension of the work of Epiphany, Orange," read an article of the time, "and will serve the social, educational and religious needs of the colored children of the Elmwood section." (Courtesy of the Episcopal Diocese of Newark.)

Christ Episcopal Church's stone church was opened in the spring of 1891 on Main Street in East Orange, replacing a wooden structure that burned down in 1888, just 20 years after its founding.

It was on St. Agnes' Day in 1904 that a delegation of Episcopalians in the Hyde Park section of East Orange called upon a visiting Bishop Edwin S. Lines and told him of the need for a church. The worshipers of what would become St. Agnes' Episcopal Church had used a clubhouse, then a barn. By 1922, a campaign was begun to build on Central Avenue a 270-seat sanctuary, which was finally consecrated on October 18, 1931. In 1956—the 25th anniversary of that event—the rector, Addison K. Groff, wrote in the parish newsletter, "The history of the church is not papers and documents alone, but the history of men, women and children. In other words, history is a living, human thing." (Courtesy of the Episcopal Diocese of Newark.)

Two

Suburban Essex and Union

Just as I am, thou wilt receive; wilt welcome, pardon, cleanse, relieve, because thy promise I believe, O Lamb of God, I come, I come

—Hymn No. 693, *The Hymnal* 1982
Composed by William Batchelder Bradbury, died 1868, Montclair, New Jersey

This depiction of Montclair's St. Luke's appeared on the cover of the church's 75th-anniversary booklet in 1935. Times were tough in 1935, as the parish's income had fallen more than 32 percent since 1930. Today its outreach includes the Second Time Around Shop and Toni's Kitchen, a food ministry for the needy. (Courtesy of the Episcopal Diocese of Newark.)

On the steps of the original Grace Episcopal Church, at Grant and Whitford Avenues in what is now Nutley, the boys' choir was ready for a morning of raised voices about a century ago. The parish, founded in 1873, built a new Norman Gothic church, designed by architect Henry P. Kirby, in 1908. The interior murals, which took English artist Clinton Balmer seven years to complete, were dedicated in June 1918. The boys are identified as, from left to right, (first row) Frost Bassford and Milton Ryan; (second row) Thomas Moffitt, Ralph Ryan, Louis Ray, and Walter Ryan; (third row) Louis MacConnaugh, Horace Bassford, Fred Gilmore, and Charles Tansley; (fourth row) Milton Witbeck, crucifer Conrad Ray, Joseph Barnes, and Charles Bassford; (fifth row) Albert Weischedel, James Barnes, and Arch Coe; (sixth row) Charles Page, Fred Young, Chester Barron, Curtis Prout, and Herbert Brandreth. (Courtesy of Grace Episcopal Church, Nutley.)

An eagle-eyed boy, front center, peers at the cameraman in this picture of Grace Church School in Nutley, taken in October 1925. It is a piece of a much larger wide-angle picture showing hundreds of pupils, another portion of which appears of the cover of this pictorial history. A couple months later, in December 1925, a fire believed to have started in faulty wiring beneath the organ destroyed the roof and its murals, the organ, and the pews. The original artist, Clinton Balmer, discovered the loss of the murals while on a subway. "Riding in the subway, strap-hanging, overlooking a neighbor's Daily News, I read vivid headlines 'Ten Years of His Life Wasted' and saw a picture of a burning building, which I recognized as Grace Church, Nutley. Then I realized that the poor strap-hanger whose 10 years of life had been wasted must be me," he said. So he undertook a second set of murals, working from 1926 to 1929 to complete them. "To this day, they remain a source of pride and joy," reads a history of the parish penned for the 125th anniversary in 1998, during the tenure of Rev. Pamela Bakal. (Courtesy of Grace Episcopal Church, Nutley.)

Rev. Deacon Wallace "Buck" Coursen instructs his young charges in the boys' choir at Christ Episcopal Church in Bloomfield/Glen Ridge. This undated photograph is one of many that now hang in the choir room of the church, which straddles the border of the two Essex County communities. (Courtesy of Christ Episcopal Church, Bloomfield and Glen Ridge.)

Rev. Edwin Augustine White preached a history-filled sermon to mark the 50th anniversary of Christ Church of Bloomfield and Glen Ridge in 1910. It was filled with stories of a seemingly endless succession of rectors, as well as one about strife in the 1870s over a "ritual" that was disturbing the church at large. "A red altar cloth was presented to the church," he said. "It was used only one Sunday, we are told, for one of the wardens, filled with indignation at the Rome-ward tendencies of the rector, entered the church on the following day and tore that Romish rag from the altar." (Courtesy of the Episcopal Diocese of Newark.)

1916 1931

The Fifteenth Anniversary
Trinity Church
(St. Luke's Parish)

North Willow Street and Glenridge Avenue
Montclair, New Jersey

The Reverend Luke M. White, D.D., Rector
The Reverend Edward Cosbey, Assistant
The Reverend George Marshal Plaskett, Vicar

The 15th anniversary of Trinity Church on Montclair's North Willow Street was a time of celebration in 1931. The parish, which found a permanent home with the assistance of St. Luke's, Montclair, in a converted armory where cavalry officers once drilled, was, like the nation, just entering the depths of the Great Depression. "With virtually none of its members employed, Trinity purchased an organ for $5,000. This is still considered a modern miracle," one parish historian later wrote. The congregation was largely made up of immigrants from the West Indies and Bermuda. (Courtesy of the Episcopal Diocese of Newark.)

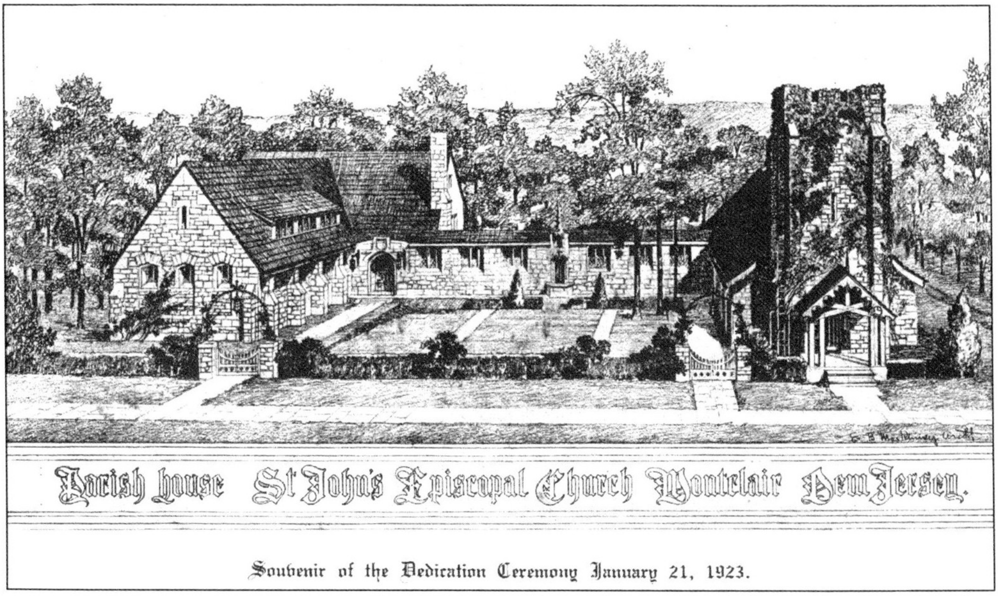

On May 14, 1921, a contingent from St. John's Episcopal Church in Montclair was at the Newark local assembly of the Brotherhood of St. Andrew. The first service of St. John's Episcopal Church, in 1896, was in a vacant storefront on Walnut Street opposite Christopher Street, but by 1901, a new church rose on Montclair Avenue at Chestnut Street. In 1923, souvenirs could be had for the dedication of the parish house. (Courtesy of the Episcopal Diocese of Newark.)

The first vested choir of St. James' Episcopal Church in Montclair processes in 1898—a decade after the founding of the parish—in an image similar to one that appeared in the 50th anniversary booklet of 1938. It was late in 1898 that the vestry named a committee to explore the use of electricity for lighting and for operating the organ's blower. "The organ had always been blown by hand, at times much to the disgust of the organist when the air failed because the sexton was sleepy," said the account in the anniversary booklet. The tower of St. James' Episcopal Church in Montclair was designed by parishioner and architect Francis A. Nelson. (Courtesy of St. James, Montclair.)

Upper Montclair Village's Bellevue Avenue is the backdrop for these hefty bells about to make their way to the tower of St. James' Episcopal Church. The largest of the bells carries this inscription: "Gloria in Excelsis Deo, This Chime of Bells Is a Memorial of the Men of St. James' Parish Who Gave Their Lives for the Freedom of the World and a Thank Offering for the

Return of Those Others Who Served 1919." Bells two through eight carry inscriptions of the seven who died. The remaining three bells are inscribed with the doxology, whose opening line is "Praise God, from Whom all blessings flow." (Courtesy of St. James, Montclair.)

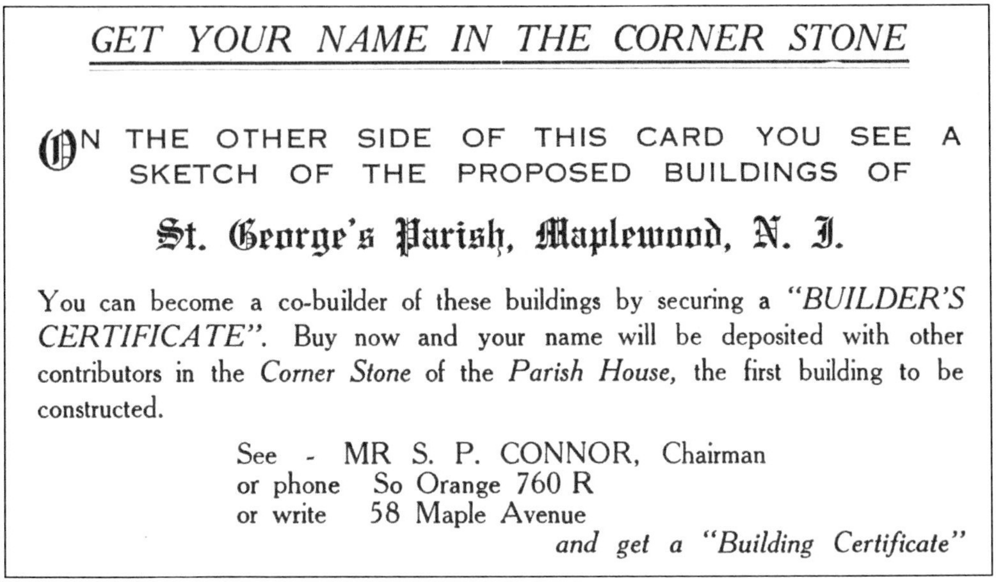

GET YOUR NAME IN THE CORNER STONE

ON THE OTHER SIDE OF THIS CARD YOU SEE A SKETCH OF THE PROPOSED BUILDINGS OF

St. George's Parish, Maplewood, N. J.

You can become a co-builder of these buildings by securing a *"BUILDER'S CERTIFICATE"*. Buy now and your name will be deposited with other contributors in the *Corner Stone* of the *Parish House,* the first building to be constructed.

See - MR S. P. CONNOR, Chairman
or phone So Orange 760 R
or write 58 Maple Avenue

and get a "Building Certificate"

At St. George's Episcopal Church in Maplewood, the parish newsletter is called *Dragon Tales*, taking its name from the story of its patron saint—and England's—St. George, who faithfully made the sign of the cross as he subdued a dragon in front of the king and queen. As an enticement to immortalize the feats of others, its building campaign in 1925 came up with a chance to become a part of history by getting one's name in the cornerstone. To this day, the parish has a living connection to history. One of its parishioners is Ulysses Grant Dietz, a great-great-grandson of Ulysses S. Grant, the victorious Civil War commander and the 18th president of the United States. (Courtesy of the Episcopal Diocese of Newark.)

St. Peter's Episcopal Church in Livingston was the original dream of its sole benefactor, Alexander Livingston Kean, who was a descendant of Gov. William Livingston, the first governor of New Jersey and the man for whom Livingston Township was named. St. Peter's Chapel, below, built by Alexander Kean as a temporary place of worship, was a prefabricated structure made in sections and held together with nuts and bolts. It was erected on the church's present site on East Mount Pleasant Avenue, on property covered with wild strawberries and known as Strawberry Hill. In 1961, the groundbreaking for a new church, above, was captured in a photograph taken by the wife of Wayne Headley, who forwarded her pictures to the diocese for its collection. (Courtesy of the Episcopal Diocese of Newark.)

First services were up two flights of stairs in a Masonic temple, then in a rented storefront, at 522 Bloomfield Avenue in Verona. By December 1929, with the great stock market crash still a vivid memory and the Great Depression still in its infancy, a building fund for a chapel was begun for the Episcopal Church of the Holy Spirit, at Gould Street and Reid Place, shown here in 1935. A large wing for a full-sized sanctuary, to the north of the chapel, was designed by architect John T. Simpson of Newark and envisioned in 1932 but took decades to become a reality. In the 1940s, Rev. Louis P. Nissen, vicar, stands with parishioners on the chapel's steps. (Courtesy of Church of the Holy Spirit, Verona.)

The Episcopal Church of the Holy Spirit's Reverend Nissen is surrounded by the youth choir in the 1940s. Reverend Nissen arrived in 1943 at the church, which was designed to conform to the lines of the nearby Verona Civic Center. (Courtesy of the Episcopal Church of the Holy Spirit, Verona; photograph by R. Kenneth Grobholz.)

"In the New York World's Fair of 1939, there will be a little bit of everything—including religion," read a magazine article of the day. And so it was on July 15, 1940, the choir of the Episcopal Church Holy Spirit in Verona sang in a concert at the fair's Temple of Religion pavilion. The choir's director was Graydon R. Clark. (Courtesy of the Episcopal Church of the Holy Spirit, Verona; photograph by Marie Higginson.)

Bishop Leland Stark came to St. Peter's Church in Essex Fells on March 20, 1955, for his first confirmation at the Essex County parish, whose roots can be traced to 1893. The class was then the largest to date for the parish, whose seal includes the image of a clenched fist holding a cross to honor the "Fighting Parson" of Revolutionary War fame, Rev. James Caldwell. The bishop is flanked by St. Peter's rector, Rev. Harold Onderdonk, to his right, and Rev. Norman Rice, assistant. (Courtesy of the Episcopal Diocese of Newark.)

St. Stephen's Church, formally consecrated on July 24, 1855, in Millburn, was designed by J. W. Priest in the American Gothic style. The New York architects Priest and H. M. Congdon also had a hand in renovations at Baltimore's St. Luke's Episcopal Church, where in 1858 they handled the additions of transepts and a chancel. The church seats 300 and is little altered except for the organ, which blocks the five rear windows. In 1961, the cornerstone was laid for a new church house at the locale. Tucked inside were such items as an 1862 Bible that was carried in the Civil War by Benjamin Livingston; it was said to have saved his life from enemy fire, with a bullet hole still visible in its jacket. Christ Church in the Short Hills section, below, started small and was enlarged many times. A bell tower that once graced the church is gone, but the bell remains in a memorial garden. (Courtesy of the Episcopal Diocese of Newark.)

Calvary, Summit's first church of any denomination, stands at Woodland Avenue around 1903, above, and in a pre-1925 photograph. Calvary retains some remnants from an earlier version of the church, which on January 8, 1893, was reduced to a charred ruin after the rector and the sexton lighted gas lamps for the morning service, only to see the Christmas trees catch fire. The parish house, completed in 1894, was constructed with many of the stones from the burned church. Two years later, this 750-seat church became a reality. (Courtesy of the Episcopal Diocese of Newark.)

Three

BERGEN AND HUDSON

Day by day, dear Lord, of thee three things I pray:
To see thee more clearly, love thee more dearly,
Follow thee more nearly, day by day.

—Hymn No. 654, The Hymnal 1982

Seen here is Westwood's Grace Episcopal Church in its early days, along the dirt road of Harrington Avenue. (Courtesy of Grace Episcopal Church, Westwood.)

Nelson Penfield is the crucifer standing behind St. Agnes' Choir at Christ Church, Hackensack, about 1939. Also gathered outside the large wood doors are Marilyn Essertier, upper right corner, and Nancy Russell, lower right corner. (Courtesy of Christ Church, Hackensack.)

The choir members of Christ Church in Hackensack grasp their hymnals and offertory music on October 20, 1957. (Courtesy of Christ Church, Hackensack.)

Arts and crafts were part of the Sunday school activities on November 13, 1960, at Christ Church, Hackensack. (Courtesy of Christ Church, Hackensack.)

In what was described as a "Little Italy" in Hackensack, residents were ever hopeful in 1914 that their petitions to the Roman Catholic Archdiocese of Newark to create their own neighborhood church would be heard. Instead the archdiocese said St. Mary's Roman Catholic Church would have to suffice and refused to send an Italian priest to organize an Italian parish. Rev. Anthony G. Lenza was informed of their predicament and soon established an "independent" church of St. Anthony of Padua against the orders of his ecclesiastical superiors. Father Lenza was immediately suspended from his priestly duties but nevertheless ministered to the neophyte congregation until "formidable opposition and financial crises" forced its closing in 1924, according to a history of the parish. The next year, the Protestant Episcopal Diocese of Newark took the congregation under its wing. Here a kindergarten class and a boys' class enjoy the early days of the newly formed Episcopal mission. (Courtesy of the Episcopal Diocese of Newark.)

There is something particularly sentimental about St. Mark's Episcopal Church in Teaneck. The 650-pound Neely bell ringing at St. Mark's Episcopal Church today was a gift from Lillian and John Mursch in 1946. It is the same bell that rang on their wedding day in 1917 at St. Luke's Church in Utica, New York. In 1937, a new parish house created room for the Sunday school, but the flourishing parish forced church and parish house to switch roles. By 1942, the parish house was equipped for church services and the original chapel was turned into a parish house. (Courtesy of the Episcopal Diocese of Newark.)

In 1965, Christ Episcopal Church in Ridgewood marked its 100th anniversary under longtime rector Alfred J. Miller, who had arrived at the parish a year before its 75th anniversary. "The rector's liberal theology and expository preaching . . . have attracted many people," the 100th anniversary brochure read. (Courtesy of the Episcopal Diocese of Newark.)

On Maywood's Oak Avenue, little Diane Read is about to cross the street to attend Sunday school at St. Martin's Episcopal Church. With her were two well-known Maywood girls, identical twins Edna and Eileen Reeke of 221 Prospect Street. The girls appeared at the 1939–1940 New York world's fair as the "Doublemint Chewing Gum" twins. "Dressing alike . . . never causes them any battles, they insist, because they like the very same clothes," said a feature story on the twins in the *Bergen Evening Record* on February 25, 1939. During that same era, Diane and her brother Jack take some time out on the steps of St. Martin's Episcopal Church. (Courtesy of the Read family.)

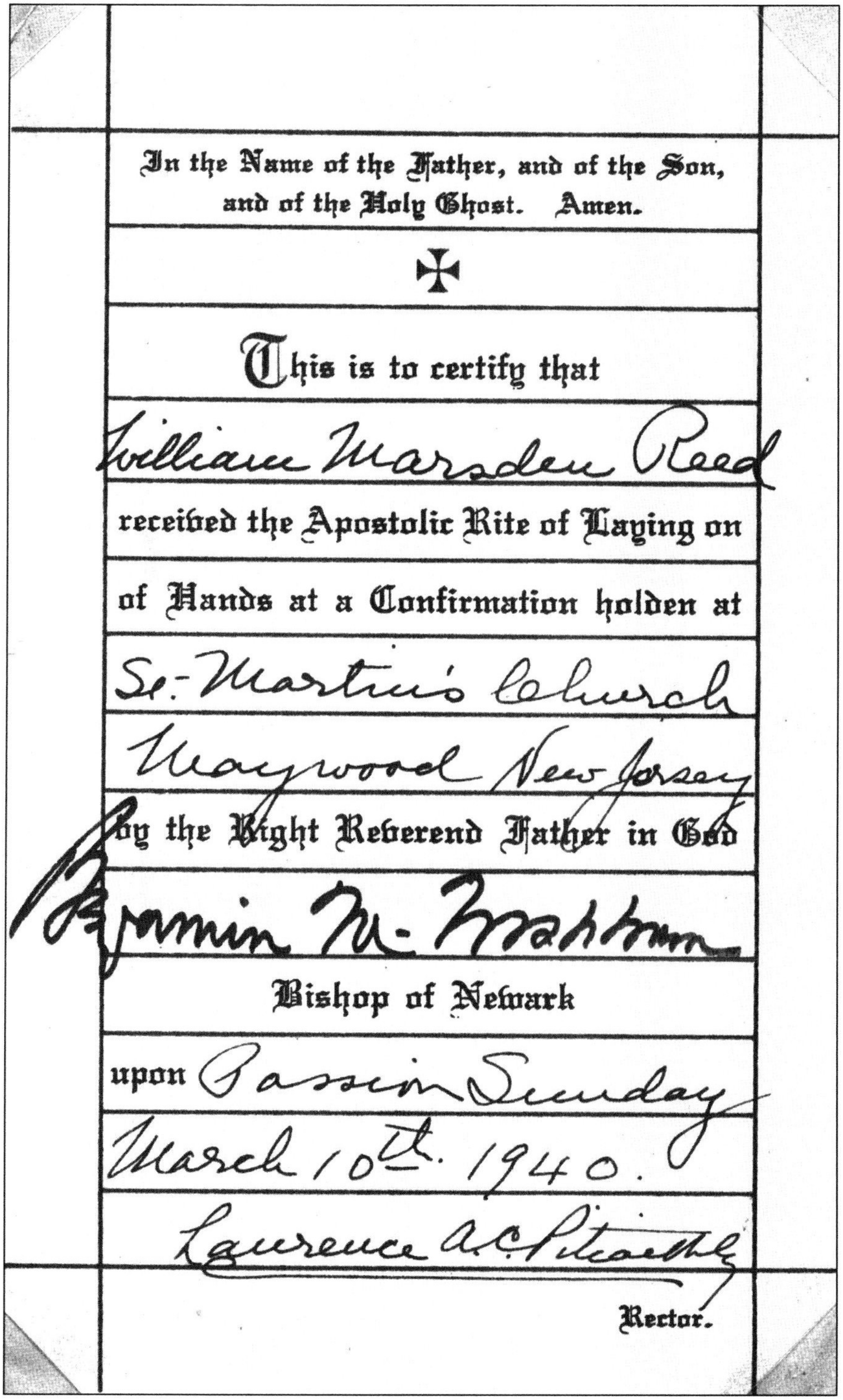
In the Name of the Father, and of the Son, and of the Holy Ghost. Amen.

✠

This is to certify that

William Marsden Reed

received the Apostolic Rite of Laying on of Hands at a Confirmation holden at

St. Martin's Church Maywood New Jersey

by the Right Reverend Father in God

Benjamin M. Washburn

Bishop of Newark

upon Passion Sunday March 10th 1940.

Laurence A. C. Pitcaithly

Rector.

Confirmation cards, carrying the signature of the bishop, have not changed much in decades. This one was awarded at St. Martin's Episcopal Church in Maywood to an altar boy by the name of William Marsden Read III. (Courtesy of the Read family.)

During the tenure of Rev. Francis S. Bancroft III, from 1960 to 2000, this delegation from St. James', Ridgefield, gathered for the diocesan convention as the Bergen County mission became a parish. The people are identified as, from left to right, (first row) William Van Dyne, Theodore Deubel, Louis Pratt, Isabelle Koeppen, Mrs. Homer Holland, Mrs. Arthur Glogan, and Arthur Glogan; (second row) Homer Holland, Bernard Snyder, Mrs. Theodore Deubel, Mrs. Fred Acker, Janet DeCarnis, Frances Lefferts, Brenda Book, Mrs. Walter White, Mrs. William Taylor, and Mrs. Louis Pratt; (third row) William Drexler, Mrs. Fred Miller, the Venerable Sydney Grant, Alice Olwig, Bishop Leland Stark, Reverend Bancroft, Bishop George Rath, Mrs. Vito DeCarnis, and Jane Van Dyne. (Courtesy of the Episcopal Diocese of Newark.)

St. James Episcopal Church of Ridgefield in 2008 marked its 140th anniversary—and the 100th anniversary of its current sanctuary—with Rt. Rev. Mark M. Beckwith, bishop, presiding. The next Sunday, the parish observed the Holy Eucharist using the 1789 Book of Common Prayer, which was used by St. James Episcopal Church's first parishioners in 1868. In the mid-20th century, a crowd came out for the Mothers and Daughters Communion Breakfast on Mothers Day. (Courtesy of the Episcopal Diocese of Newark.)

A new St. Matthew's Episcopal Church rose on Spring Valley Road in Paramus after this picture appeared on the cover of the 1956 *Building Fund Canvass*. "Increased giving—as has been proved so many times over—will develop greatly increased interest in our Church and in our spiritual lives," wrote the authors. (Courtesy of the Episcopal Diocese of Newark.)

The Church of the Epiphany in Allendale was founded in 1872 and often wound up outgrowing its space, resulting in the "shed style" replacement, with recessed entrance, consecrated in 1979 at 55 George Street. In 1954, the young vicar Bayard Hancock was keenly aware of the growth amid the height of the baby boom. "We have the youngsters every place but hanging from the chandeliers," he told reporter Wilma Supik, "and believe me, if the chandeliers were stronger, they'd be up there too!" (Courtesy of the Episcopal Diocese of Newark.)

The wedding day of Rev. Worthington Campbell of St. Paul's Episcopal Church in Montvale and Dorothy Fave drew a crowd on June 26, 1954, not the least of which was St. Paul's choir, as well as Bishop Noble C. Powell of Maryland, John Heuss, and Bishop Benjamin M. Washburn. The locale across the Hudson River was Trinity Church in the heart of New York's Financial District. (Courtesy of the Episcopal Diocese of Newark.)

The production was called *Musicale* and included such tunes as the "Bells of St. Mary"; "People Will Say We're in Love," a duet by young Phyllis Greve and Walter Ratcliff; and the "Barber of Seville," with baritone David Hughes. On January 31, 1948, the program for the Holy Trinity (Hillsdale) Episcopal Church Choir Club event was packed with advertisements from merchants, including the Westwood Bakery and Everett's Grocery. Here the cast is captured on film by a photographer for R. J. Mason Studio. (Courtesy of Holy Trinity, Hillsdale, and Gail Bates.)

The laying of the cornerstone for a new parish hall at St. John's Episcopal Church in Ramsey came with a prayer from Bishop Benjamin M. Washburn on January 29, 1956. (Courtesy of the Episcopal Diocese of Newark.)

The predecessor of today's Church of the Good Shepherd, Christ Chapel in Midland Park, seen above, rose in 1909 on a lot donated by the Granite Linen Company in a neighborhood known as Wortendyke. It was not until 36 years later that the newspapers announced "Church Mortgage Goes Up in Flames" over a photograph of the occasion. At that ceremony are, from left to right, Canon W. O. Leslie; Rev. George S. Bowden, rector; Bishop Benjamin M. Washburn; and, in front, Kenneth W. MacDonald, church treasurer, and Harold Nelson, vestryman. The last service in the old church was on September 2, 1962, but its cornerstone was reclaimed for use in a new sanctuary. (Courtesy of the Episcopal Diocese of Newark.)

Within a year of its 1895 founding, the Episcopalians of Hasbrouck Heights witnessed a name change: the Episcopal Church of the Beloved Disciple became the Episcopal Church of St. John the Divine. The next year, the parish obtained a one-story frame schoolhouse as a place for worship, which by its 50th anniversary had been converted into a "residential bungalow." In 1925, the fund-raising drive to erect a new church was launched. (Courtesy of the Episcopal Diocese of Newark.)

In July 1925, this rendering was created for St. Bartholomew's Protestant Episcopal Church in Ho-Ho-Kus, at Franklin Turnpike and Elmwood Drive. The architectural firm was Henry J. McGill and Talbot F. Hamlin of New York City. By 1934, amid the Great Depression, Hamlin was compelled to seek work outside the field and became Avery architecture librarian at Columbia University, eventually teaching there until his death in 1956. (Courtesy of the Episcopal Diocese of Newark.)

At the consecration of All Saints in Leonia in 1922, actually founded in 1893, joyful parishioners sang a well-known hymn as a recessional. "Glorious things of thee are spoken, Zion, city of our God. He whose word cannot be broken, Formed thee for his own abode; On the Rock of Ages founded, What can shake thy sure repose?" Nothing could shake the parish from its Park Avenue church. By the 75th anniversary, in 1968, the rector, Rev. Norman Spicer, noted a discussion to erect a new church, an idea that was declined. "The unanimous vote at the annual parish meeting was to preserve and beautify the building that has been the scene of so many joyous and happy ceremonies as well as sad farewells for families and friends." (Courtesy of the Episcopal Diocese of Newark.)

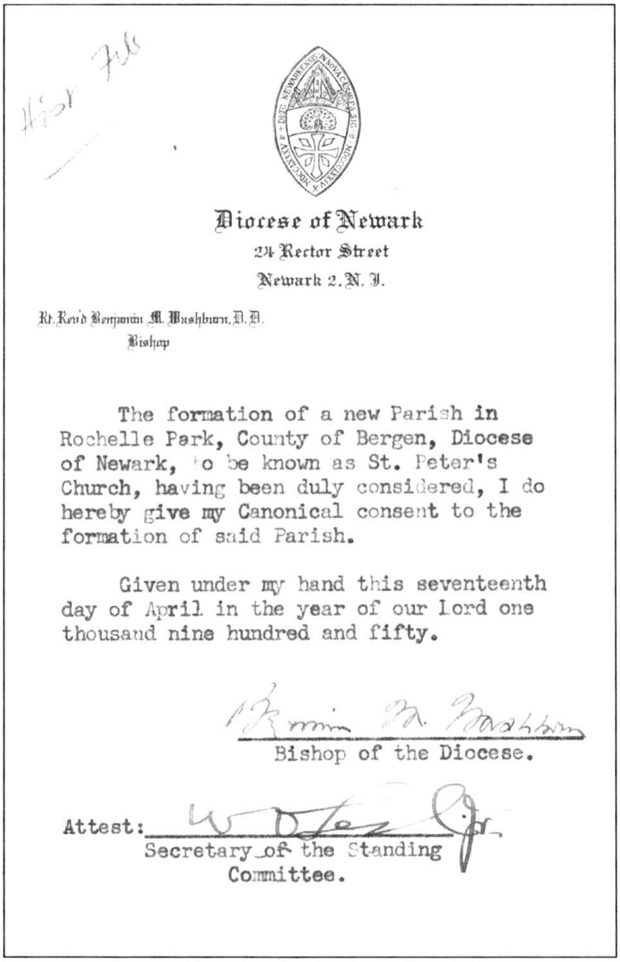

Diocese of Newark
24 Rector Street
Newark 2, N. J.

Rt. Rev'd Benjamin M. Washburn, D. D.
Bishop

The formation of a new Parish in Rochelle Park, County of Bergen, Diocese of Newark, to be known as St. Peter's Church, having been duly considered, I do hereby give my Canonical consent to the formation of said Parish.

Given under my hand this seventeenth day of April in the year of our Lord one thousand nine hundred and fifty.

Benjamin M. Washburn
Bishop of the Diocese.

Attest: W. D. ... Jr.
Secretary of the Standing Committee.

In 1950, St. Peter's Episcopal Church in Rochelle Park transitioned from mission to parish, prompting a formal letter from Rt. Rev. Benjamin M. Washburn, bishop. A few years later, Rev. Harold N. Cutler was conducting four services each Sunday, leading to plans for a bigger church. Life, though, had its distractions. For Cutler, that meant a collection of 300 tropical fish in 15 tanks lining the walls of half of his kitchen. Many became gifts as pets to children. "I also minister to local fish," Cutler joked to a reporter for the *Bergen Evening Record*. (Courtesy of the Episcopal Diocese of Newark.)

In 1946, Rt. Rev. Benjamin M. Washburn, bishop of Newark, came to the Church of the Ascension in Bogota for the ordination to the diaconate of Charles Edward Sutton, right, who became the first resident vicar of a mission established in 1921. The event was captured by photographer Louis G. Gill of Teaneck. Later, in 1947, Sutton would be ordained to the priesthood in the same sanctuary. By 1951, the year of the burning of the church mortgage, he had this to say to his parish: "Merely reading the names of devoted parishioners of past times, of clergy and laity devoted to the Mission, will not suffice. We must show our real appreciation of their self-sacrifice by making this 30th Anniversary not an end, but a beginning." (Courtesy of the Episcopal Diocese of Newark.)

In the Bergen County community of Glen Rock, the original All Saints Chapel was dedicated on All Saints Day in 1919, some six years after its beginning. By 1960, a modern church rose in its stead to accommodate a communicant list approaching the 1,000 mark. Today the parish's Web site touts its "Radical Welcome" and quotes from St. Benedict to make the point: "All guests who present themselves are to be welcomed as Christ Himself." (Courtesy of the Episcopal Diocese of Newark.)

All Saints Episcopal Church in Bergenfield marked its 100th anniversary in 2007, with a visit from Rt. Rev. Mark M. Beckwith, the newly consecrated bishop of Newark. The November 4 service at the church, at North Washington and West Central Avenues, featured the rededication of a large processional cross that had been out of service for nearly a decade. (Courtesy of the Episcopal Diocese of Newark.)

You are cordially invited to attend the ceremony of

The Burning of the Mortgage

of

St. Paul's Church and Parish Hall

Sunset Avenue and York Road, North Arlington, N. J.

at a Service of Evening Prayer and Sermon

to be held on

Sunday, December 17th, 1944 at 8:00 P. M.

The Address will be delivered by The Right Reverend

Benjamin M. Washburn, D. D.

Bishop of Newark

A Social Hour will be held following the Service

in the Parish Hall

It was always worthy of a printed invitation. The "Burning of the Mortgage" at St. Paul's, North Arlington and elsewhere, was a welcome event, worthy of a visit by the bishop. (Courtesy of the Episcopal Diocese of Newark.)

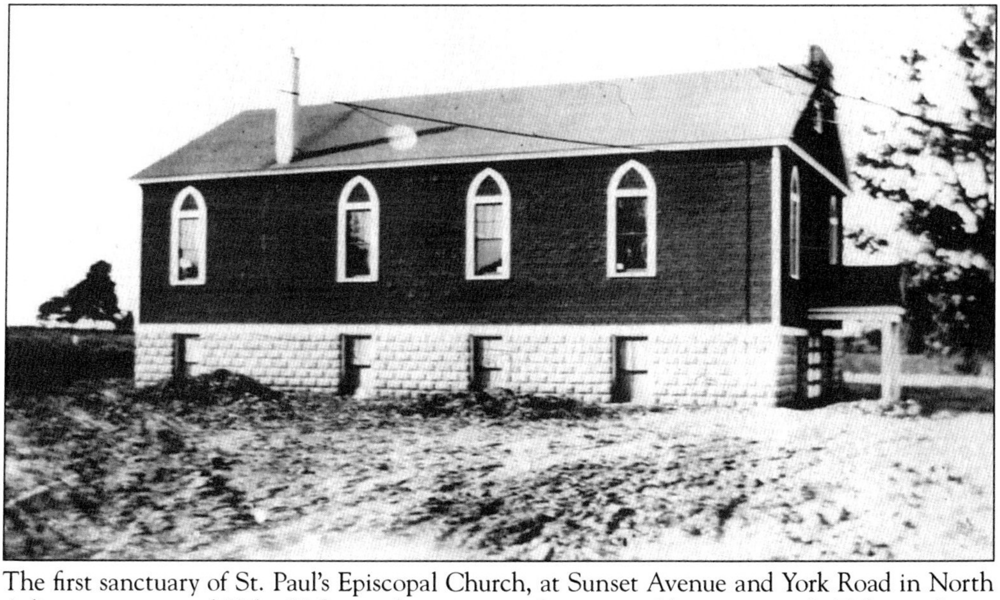

The first sanctuary of St. Paul's Episcopal Church, at Sunset Avenue and York Road in North Arlington, measured 32 by 54 feet and sat atop an aboveground basement with 10-foot ceilings, according to notes by the diocese's archdeacon in 1915. William Martin was the minister in charge. The church began as a mission in 1914 at the home of Mrs. Edgar Ward with an attendance of four. A decade later, the $12,000 job to move the church to a new foundation at the property's rear was underway. (Courtesy of the Episcopal Diocese of Newark.)

Walter M. Schirra Jr. was the only astronaut to have flown Mercury, Gemini, and Apollo missions. But on October 3, 1962, the day of his launch as pilot of the Sigma 7 Mercury flight, he was being remembered as the boy who attended the Church of the Annunciation in the Bergen County community of Oradell, at left. "He was a fine Sunday school student, served on the altar and was very helpful in all of our church activities," Rev. Louis Jones said on the day of Schirra's 17,557-mile-per-hour trip in orbit. The church, which traces its beginnings to 1901, took its name from the holy day closest to its founding, the Feast of the Annunciation. The Hackensack-born Schirra, who died in 2007, was one of the original seven Mercury astronauts named by NASA in 1959. (Courtesy of the Episcopal Diocese of Newark.)

Trinity Church, Cliffside Park, sits on a high bluff above the Hudson River, overlooking Manhattan. Today the church's nickname is the "Cathedral of the Palisades." Trinity has had parish status for more than 70 years. (Courtesy of the Episcopal Diocese of Newark.)

The Gothic-style St. Paul's Episcopal Church in Englewood, pictured in the 1960s, was erected in 1899 using rose limestone from the original 1866 sanctuary. Its stained-glass windows are from Tiffany La Farge and Lamb Studios. (Courtesy of the Episcopal Diocese of Newark.)

The renovated St. Clement's Episcopal Church in Hawthorne reopened in 1936 and still looks very much the same, other than the addition of brick, stained-glass windows, and a more substantial bell tower. Change, as always, was constant. In 1957, the parish newsletter the *Tidings* carried a farewell letter from the beloved rector, Rev. Leon H. Plante, after seven years at the parish's helm. "For all that He has given to me, I give thanks," he wrote, "for all that He has given to you because of me, I give thanks; for all that He has given me, because of you, I give thanks; for all that He has allowed us to do, in His Name, I give thanks." (Courtesy of the Episcopal Diocese of Newark.)

The original building of the Church of the Mediator, right, stood on Edgewater's River Road. In 1855, it was called the Edgewater Chapel and sat atop land later occupied by the Aluminum Company of America, according to a history penned in 1957. The original rectory, below, was completed in 1867, built of lumber from the soldiers' barracks at Sandy Hook and consequently known as the "Rectory Militant." (Courtesy of the Episcopal Diocese of Newark.)

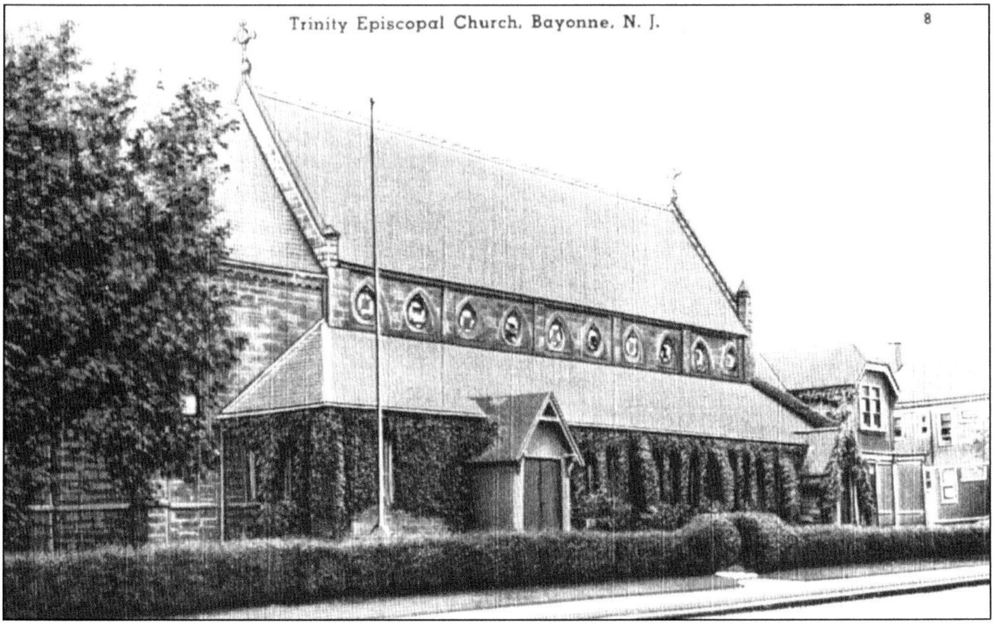

The first sanctuary of Trinity Episcopal Church in Bayonne was destroyed by fire in 1879, as was this 1881 stone version, designed by architects Stent and Sargents. When a fire destroyed that church, there was thought if disbanding, but perseverance prevailed, and a new church was opened in 1974. (Courtesy of the Episcopal Diocese of Newark.)

Rev. W. J. Tilley was vicar of Christ Church in Harrison, which was in Hudson County but more closely aligned with Newark, its Essex County neighbor across the river, beginning in 1893. His tenure was one of "energetic but kindly leadership," according to a *History of the Episcopal Church in Essex County, New Jersey*. The publication was created for the Bazaar for St. Barnabas Hospital in 1908. (Courtesy of the Episcopal Diocese of Newark.)

New members of the Girls Friendly Society (GFS) are mostly smiles on the steps of Trinity Episcopal Church, Kearny, on May 11, 1941. Joining the new inductees were Rev. Warren Filkens, who had a lengthy tenure of nearly 30 years at the parish. Also on hand were Mrs. Fitt and Miss E. Kennedy, according to the inscription on the photograph. The GFS, founded in 1875 in England by Mary Elizabeth Townsend, is believed to be the first organization for women in the Church of England. The GFS and its motto live on today. "To share God's love for all people, to worship and serve faithfully," it reads. "To make my words true, and my actions right, to grow strong in mind, body, and spirit, To make the world a better place to live." (Courtesy of Trinity Episcopal Church, Kearny, and Rev. Rose Hassan.)

Thelma Coleman spends time with her charges at Trinity Episcopal Church, Arlington-Kearny, in the early 1950s during the tenure of Rev. Frank Coleman, who arrived in 1948 via New Brunswick, Canada. By 1987, the parish's centennial, the congregants sized up their lot this way: "We like to think of our congregation as one large family, where one helps another on an individual level, where support can be found when needed, and happiness shared by all." (Courtesy of Trinity Episcopal Church, Kearny, and Rev. Rose Hassan.)

A rite of spring for any bishop is confirmation. Such was the case on April 3, 1955, in Union City as Bishop Benjamin M. Washburn greeted the newest full-fledged members of the flock. (Courtesy of the Episcopal Diocese of Newark.)

St. Paul's Episcopal Church in Bergen, Jersey City, is seen as it looked in 1861, a year after its founding. Milestones at the Duncan Avenue church, communicated via *St. Paul's Chronicle*, included the rebuilding and expansion of the church in the late 1880s. By 1946, electronically controlled carillon chimes—dedicated as a memorial given by vestryman James E. Pope—were in place, producing chimes that could be heard six miles from the tower, according to a 1948 article in the *Jersey Observer*. (Courtesy of the Episcopal Diocese of Newark.)

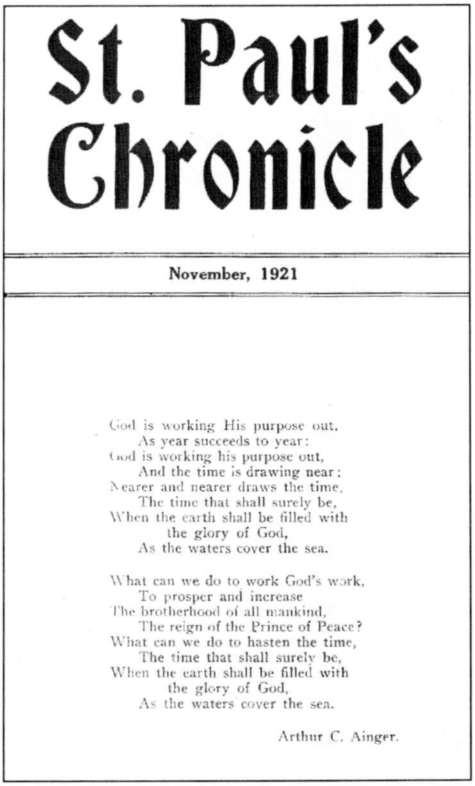

St. Paul's Chronicle

November, 1921

God is working His purpose out,
As year succeeds to year:
God is working his purpose out,
And the time is drawing near:
Nearer and nearer draws the time,
The time that shall surely be,
When the earth shall be filled with
the glory of God,
As the waters cover the sea.

What can we do to work God's work,
To prosper and increase
The brotherhood of all mankind,
The reign of the Prince of Peace?
What can we do to hasten the time,
The time that shall surely be,
When the earth shall be filled with
the glory of God,
As the waters cover the sea.

Arthur C. Ainger.

Their slogan was "Once a Trinity Choir Boy, always a Trinity Choir Boy," so on Sunday, May 10, 1925, these choristers gathered for the sixth service of the Trinity Choir Alumni of Hoboken's Trinity Episcopal Church, then under the spiritual guidance of Rev. Malcolm A. Shipley. The alumni choir, organized in 1919, had more than 300 names on its roster, with members whose tenure in some cases dated from 1876. (Courtesy of the Episcopal Diocese of Newark.)

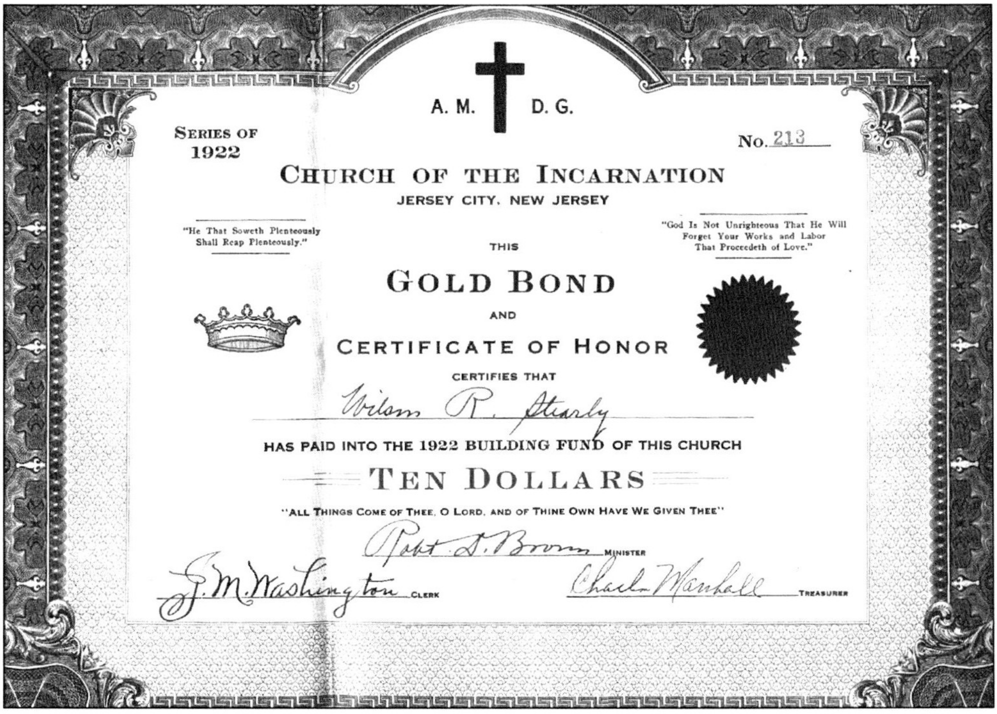

A. M. D. G.

SERIES OF 1922

No. 213

CHURCH OF THE INCARNATION

JERSEY CITY, NEW JERSEY

"He That Soweth Plenteously Shall Reap Plenteously."

"God Is Not Unrighteous That He Will Forget Your Works and Labor That Proceedeth of Love."

THIS

GOLD BOND

AND

CERTIFICATE OF HONOR

CERTIFIES THAT

Wilson R. Stearly

HAS PAID INTO THE 1922 BUILDING FUND OF THIS CHURCH

TEN DOLLARS

"ALL THINGS COME OF THEE, O LORD, AND OF THINE OWN HAVE WE GIVEN THEE"

Robt. D. Brown MINISTER

J. M. Washington CLERK

Charles Marshall TREASURER

The "Gold Bond"—in this case issued to Wilson Stearly, bishop—was awarded to those who contributed to the building fund of the Church of the Incarnation in Jersey City, an African American parish whose roots date from 1910. By 1928, ground was broken for the mission on Storms Avenue. (Courtesy of the Episcopal Diocese of Newark.)

The "Mother Church" of Jersey City's Episcopal churches, Grace Church Van Vorst in Jersey City, dates from 1847 and flourished in the beginning of the last century, until the Great Depression and the outward migration of well-to-do families. In 1933, it would begin a 32-year stretch without a rector and by World War II was operated by members of the Church Army. Come the postwar years, two young priests and seminarian took up the challenge to "work directly with the underprivileged" in a "deteriorating urban community." Among them was Paul Moore Jr., whose wife, Jenny McKean Moore, in 1968, published an account of their decade together in the slums, *The People on Second Street*. Later ministers of Grace Church Van Vorst conduct a street-corner service at Jersey Avenue and Second Street in an updated photograph. (Courtesy of the Episcopal Diocese of Newark.)

"Year by year, babies and sometimes their mothers are baptized in this place," read a 1928 article on St. Katharine's Home, run by the Sisters of St. Margaret. The retreat, at 32 Reservoir Avenue in Jersey City Heights, was founded in 1893. "St. Katharine's Home . . . has done meritorious work in helping unmarried girls who have been led astray for the first time and sheltering them before and after motherhood," the article said. (Courtesy of the Episcopal Diocese of Newark.)

Four

MORRIS AND PASSAIC

Al-le-lu-ia, al-le-lu-ia! Give thanks to the ris-en Lord.
Al-le-lu-ia, al-le-lu-ia! Give praise to his Name.
. . . Come, let us praise the liv-ing God,
Joy-ful-ly sing to our Sa-vior.

—Hymn No. 178, *The Hymnal* 1982

In 1906, Grace Church in Madison, shown in a postcard from that year, was embarking on a new method of fund-raising, shifting away from the main income producer of pew rentals, a practice that nevertheless continued to the early 1950s. In March 1907, the vestry authorized moving to a pledge/envelope system. (Courtesy of the Episcopal Diocese of Newark.)

Ground was broken in 1887 for St. Peter's Episcopal Church in Morristown, whose origins actually date from 1791. But the lengthy creation of a campus, under the auspices of architects McKim, Meade, and White of New York, would not be finished until 1911. Back in the 1840s, a new rector arrived. He embraced the Oxford Movement and its call for the return of "high church" doctrines such as the apostolic succession, the real presence of Christ in the Eucharist, and the Catholicity of the church. All did not agree, leading in 1852 to the formation of a second Episcopal church in Morristown, the Church of the Redeemer. (Courtesy of the Episcopal Diocese of Newark.)

In 1852, the Church of the Redeemer in Morristown was founded by a breakaway group of parishioners who wanted worship other than those of the "high church" doctrines embraced by the arrival of their previous rector at St. Peter's Episcopal Church, Morristown. In time, the Church of the Redeemer's campus came to contain three stone structures: a Norman Gothic church seating 375, a two-story parish house, and a 12-room rectory. (Courtesy of the Episcopal Diocese of Newark.)

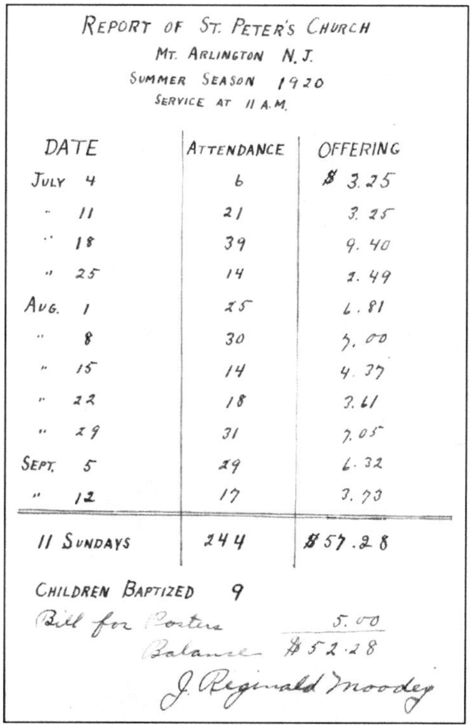

REPORT OF ST. PETER'S CHURCH
MT. ARLINGTON N. J.
SUMMER SEASON 1920
SERVICE AT 11 A.M.

DATE	ATTENDANCE	OFFERING
JULY 4	6	$ 3.25
" 11	21	3.25
" 18	39	9.40
" 25	14	2.49
AUG. 1	25	6.81
" 8	30	7.00
" 15	14	4.37
" 22	18	3.61
" 29	31	7.05
SEPT. 5	29	6.32
" 12	17	3.73
11 SUNDAYS	244	$57.28

CHILDREN BAPTIZED 9

Bill for Posters 5.00

Balance $52.28

J. Reginald Moodey

In 1920, at St. Peter's Episcopal Church in Mount Arlington, the usual record keeping showed a season-long attendance of 244 and contributions of $57.28. There were nine baptisms that summer. Today the parish bills itself as "the hugging church." (Courtesy of the Episcopal Diocese of Newark.)

This image of the choir of St. Peter's Episcopal Church in Mount Arlington appeared in an edition of the *Lake Hopatcong Breeze* in the early 1920s. The parish, in 1894, made its home at a just consecrated church at Edgemere Avenue in what was then known as Breslin Park. The land

itself, in 1889, was donated by Robert Dunlap, whose name appears in society news at the time in the *New York Times*. (Courtesy of the Episcopal Diocese of Newark.)

One of the stops on the walking tour of historic downtown Dover is the neo-Gothic St. John's Episcopal Church, completed in 1871 and listed on the New Jersey and national lists of historic places. The church, on South Bergen Street, was designed by Richard Upjohn, whose many Episcopal Church creations include Trinity Church on New York's Wall Street. On November 8, 1914, Sunday school students and faculty, as well as the youth choir, above, gathered on the east lawn of the church to mark the parish's 65th anniversary of incorporation. (Courtesy of St. John's, Dover, and Alvin Brandt.)

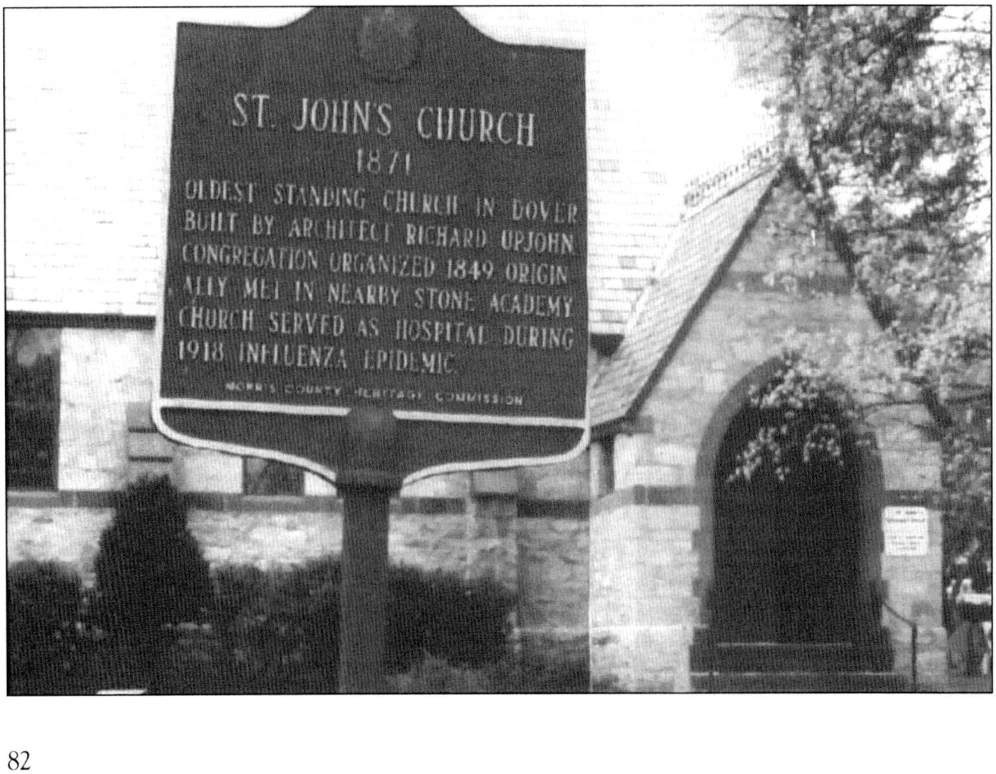

Mrs. Dodd's School House was moved to an adjoining lot to make way for St. Mark's Episcopal Church in Mendham in 1872. The parish had held its first services in the old school, but it would then become a public library. By 1930, the parish was raising money to buy a nearby storefront, below, to conduct activities for boys and girls. (Courtesy of the Episcopal Diocese of Newark.)

It was a humble beginning for the Church of the Savior in Denville, which in 1955 conducted services in the old Methodist parsonage at 77 Diamond Spring Road and then found itself conducting Sunday school classes at a public school. Soon land was purchased next to a firehouse on East Main Street, where a temporary chapel was erected, only to be lost within a year to the state for construction of Route 80. By Palm Sunday 1959, however, a new 400-seat church was dedicated on Morris Avenue. (Courtesy of the Episcopal Diocese of Newark.)

ST. PETER'S CHURCH, MOUNTAIN LAKES

In the Roaring Twenties, the grand plan for St. Peter's, Mountain Lakes, comprised a stone church with belfry tower, parish house, and rectory—all in one. "As the cost of such a group of buildings proved to be too great for the parish to carry, the design was modified," according to a history in 1948, the parish's 25th anniversary. For that 1948 milestone, parishioners were asked to send "a birthday gift" to pay down the church's debt. (Courtesy of the Episcopal Diocese of Newark.)

St. Peter's Episcopal Church

25th Anniversary—1948

Dear Rector and Vestry:

I am enclosing a check for $............ as a birthday gift to St. Peter's and to help reduce the debt* on the church.

Signed ....

Address ....

City ....

*The debt on the church is $10,000 and the total net indebtedness of the parish is $24,000.

All Saints Episcopal Church, in the Millington section of Long Hill Township, traces its roots to 1904. In its early years, under the direction of Rev. August Ahrens, the church might aptly have been called "the Church in the Wilderness," since it was surrounded by grassy growth and weeds, according to an article of the era. A vintage postcard above depicts "the first church consecrated by Bishop (Edwin Stevens) Lines" in 1906, and the image at left carries a handwritten welcome stating, "Christmas Greetings from your humble servant, August Ahrens, 1913." (Courtesy of the Episcopal Diocese of Newark.)

In 1917, St. Andrew's began in Lincoln Park, at one point early in its history paying $50 for a schoolhouse for use as a church, above, only to never actually use it. By the early 1920s, Robert Thorpe, a deacon, was advanced to the priesthood. The Liverpool-born Thorpe, then 77, had an interesting history himself. His career took him on 514 transatlantic trips as a purser on the Guion Line. Even his service in New Jersey made for notable trips. He had been commuting from his home in East Orange to Lincoln Park. "This has necessitated leaving . . . about 7:30 o'clock," read a newspaper account, "commuting to the city by trolley, taking the bus to Mountain View and changing to another bus for Boonton, where he is generally met by one of the parishioners and taken the rest of the distance by automobile." By 1958, a new church seating 300, below, became the parish's home. (Courtesy of the Episcopal Diocese of Newark.)

The modern style of St. David's Episcopal Church in Kinnelon, whose groundbreaking was on June 9, 1962, is attributed to architect Eldridge Snyder. His handiwork also can also be found at Oberlin College in Ohio, where his "modern movement" style was evident at Harkness House and other dormitories in the late 1940s and early 1950s. (Courtesy of the Episcopal Diocese of Newark.)

In 1920, St. Mark's Episcopal Church was the youngest of Paterson's five Episcopal churches, having held its first service in 1894 at the old St. Paul's Sunday school. That building was lost in the great fire of 1902, leading to the building of this edifice from 1904 to 1905 at Broadway and Straight Street. The first rector, William P. Evans (1894–1900), shared time in Clifton, helping an infant parish by the name of St. Peter's begin its mission in that neighboring city.

A "then and now" look at St. Paul's Episcopal Church in Paterson shows the original church, erected in 1825 and destroyed by fire in 1848, on land where the historic city hall stands today. Today's version, on Broadway at East Eighteenth and Van Houten Streets, below, was erected from 1893 to 1897 in what was known as the "Silk City." During the tenure of Rev. David Stuart Hamilton, from 1895 to 1938, the church school grew from less than 100 to more than 2,100 and the congregant rolls swelled from 200 to more than 2,000, making it one of the largest Episcopal congregations in the United States. Among the worshippers were many wealthy industrialists. At its 150th anniversary, on June 4, 1967, celebrants of all faiths in what had become a declining inner city sang, "A mighty fortress is our God . . . His Kingdom never faileth." (Courtesy of the Episcopal Diocese of Newark.)

Trinity Episcopal Church of Paterson, founded in 1881, built a new sanctuary in 1936 at Marion Street and Totowa Avenue. Under Rev. Charles J. Child, who served the parish for 31 years, the communicant list grew to nearly 600, which put the Tudor-style parish house, below, to good use. Trinity Episcopal Church gave birth to Christ Mission, an offspring, in Totowa. (Courtesy of the Episcopal Diocese of Newark.)

The "high altar" at Passaic's St. John's Episcopal Church, founded in 1859, was pictured for a postcard on the 85th anniversary. The Norman Gothic church, at Lafayette and Passaic Avenues, in 1915 communicated with its congregation monthly via the *Parish Gazette*. "Seats free. Strangers welcome," it proclaimed. (Courtesy of the Episcopal Diocese of Newark.)

In 1963, St. Aidan's Episcopal Mission was in a decaying section of Paterson with 1,000 children in the immediate neighborhood, many with little to do, wrote Eugene L. Avery, vicar. He spoke of the challenge of the urban ministry in a parish largely made up of domestics from the East Indies in a community where many were unchurched. But little miracles seemingly never ceased. "Two little girls brought eight new children to Sunday School, just two Sundays ago," he wrote. "The harvest truly is great, but the laborers are few." (Courtesy of the Episcopal Diocese of Newark.)

In 1944, Christ Mission in Totowa had 30 parishioners serving in the war effort. "Our faith must be as strong as theirs," a parishioner wrote during World War II. "Here is your pledge card. Fill it out, sign it, and return it to become a soldier of Christ in the front ranks!!! Are we giving more in '44!" The parishioner was handy with a camera, too, taking pictures that year of a wedding and a church school with 95 enrolled. (Courtesy of the Episcopal Diocese of Newark.)

"A friendly little church where even strangers feel at home" was how St. George's Episcopal Church was described in 1931 on its 25th anniversary. The rectory, below, fronted a park in 1921, when Rev. Theodore Andrews oversaw the Passaic mission on its 15th anniversary as well as one in Garfield. That year, the choir posed for a photograph on the day of the bishop's visit, October 2, 1921. The Monroe Street congregation, whose "mother church" was St. John's Episcopal Church of Passaic, named John De Luca as its warden in 1943 when Most Rev. Benjamin M. Washburn, bishop of Newark, came to celebrate the church's consecration. In 1949, St. Andrew's Church on Tulip Street joined St. George's Mission. (Courtesy of the Episcopal Diocese of Newark.)

At a May 23, 1963, parish meeting at St. Peter's Episcopal Church in Clifton, a close vote of 50-41 cleared the way for the building of a new sanctuary to replace a *c.* 1899 version said to be badly in need of repairs. On March 20, 1966, a "Mothering Sunday," the cornerstone was laid on Clifton Avenue, a little more than a block from downtown's main shopping strip. "We had a great outpouring of our people, including the little ones," said Rev. Louis Luisa. (Courtesy of St. Peter's Episcopal Church, Clifton.)

Back in 1981, when Rev. Jorge Gutierrez had just arrived at St. Peter's Episcopal Church in Clifton, he met a reporter by the name of Mary Flanagan. "Somewhere," he told her during an interview, "I'm sure there's a group whose needs are not being met. Maybe the church can began to meet those needs." Those words proved prophetic. For in October 1986, St. Peter's Shelter opened in the so-called memorial house, sandwiched between the church and the rectory. There families—one at a time—would be given the means to lift themselves out of homelessness. In 1996, on the church's centennial, Don Fischer, longtime warden, organist, and choir director, logged the event as one of his best remembrances. "I remember," he wrote, "the night in 1985 when the vestry approved St. Peter's Haven."

St. Stephen's Mission, in Clifton's Delawanna section, had its beginnings in 1905 and for many years had a pastoral relationship with Grace Episcopal Church in Nutley. In its prayers all along was the hope of full parish status. "The day has at last dawned when we see visions of 'The Church of St. Stephen's,'" wrote one observer in 1926. By May 1963, near the end of the parish's time at Delawanna and Linden Avenues, Canon Beach of the diocese was conducting Sunday services at the mission. "The problems are to increase the size and stewardship of the membership," Rev. F. Vernon Losee, vicar of Grace Church in East Rutherford, said in an assessment to the Venerable Sydney K. Grant, archdeacon of the diocese. Hymn No. 172, noted on the hymn board in this undated photograph, is an evening hymn in the 1940 edition of *The Hymnal*. "Now the day is over, Night is drawing nigh, Shadows of the evening, Steal across the sky," reads one verse. "When the morning wakens, Then I may arise." (Courtesy of the Episcopal Diocese of Newark.)

Five

Rural Outposts

Hail, wind, and rain, loud blowing snowstorms,
Sing to the Lord a new song!
Flowers and trees, loud rustling dry leaves,
Sing to the Lord a new song!
He has done marvelous things.
I, too, will praise him with a new song!

—Hymn No. 412, *The Hymnal* 1982

Rev. Edwin S. Ford (rear center), pictured with a Sunday school group in Hopewell, was the trailblazer of the Western Counties Mission. "When in 1919, the Rev'd Edwin S. Ford . . . took the country charge composed of Hamburg and Vernon," Bishop Wilson R. Stearly wrote in a 1931 appeal for the church extension fund, "it was with a fixed purpose to give his life to the evangelizing and building up of people in remote places in the country." (Courtesy of the Episcopal Diocese of Newark, photograph by A. J. Bloom.)

St. Luke's Episcopal Church in Hope is on the National Register of Historic Places and counts itself among the dozen most important early neo-Gothic churches in the United States. The church, according to the parish's Web site, is in a tiny village that seems to be about 150 years, rather than an hour and a half, from Manhattan. William Bulgin, a builder and craftsman from England, is reported to have worked on the construction of St. Luke's Episcopal Church in 1832. Some of the most notable features are the graceful spiral stair in the narthex and the window directly above the entrance. (Courtesy of the Episcopal Diocese of Newark.)

"Queen Provided Warren Church's Music, Plate on Hope Organ Shows Anne of England Gave It," reads the October 7, 1938, newspaper story in the *Newark Evening News*. St. Luke's Episcopal Church in Hope, it turns out, obtained the organ around 1839, some seven years after its founding. It hailed from Trinity Church in New York City, which received the organ from Queen Anne in 1713, near the end of her reign as a British monarch. (Courtesy of the Episcopal Diocese of Newark.)

In the North Jersey hills, Rev. A. F. Chillson, vicar of the Good Shepherd Mission of Ringwood Manor, administered to the needs of the people known as the "Jackson Whites," descendants of whites, African Americans, and Native Americans who lived in the poverty-stricken community. Katherine Bogert, in a newsletter sampling called "Pages from Miss Bogert's Diary," spoke of her experiences. "This evening there was a timid knock at the door and when I opened it a little voice said, 'Miss Bogert, my daddy says have you got any adhesive tape?' I gave him the last I had. I thought some suggestions might be made on my part about 'adhering' to Sunday School." (Courtesy of the Episcopal Diocese of Newark.)

The work of Good Shepherd Mission of Ringwood Manor was not unlike those of others in the diocese. In a mimeographed newsletter during the tenure of Rev. A. F. Chillson, it was described this way: "The folks turn to the church for all kinds of things. They come for first aid . . . free dental care, wanting to know how the vicar found their friends in the hospital . . . wanting to know if a mother or father is going to recover from some serious operation." Here he discusses medical needs with "Grandma Van Dunk," the colony's midwife. (Courtesy of the Episcopal Diocese of Newark.)

On September 28, 1958, the sermon hymn sung on the occasion of the 125th anniversary of St. Mary's Episcopal Church in Belvidere was a familiar one: "Glorious Things of Thee Are Spoken." The church illustrated here, known as Zion Episcopal Church until 1954, was built in 1901. The parish today in the western New Jersey town draws worshipers from adjoining Pennsylvania. (Courtesy of the Episcopal Diocese of Newark.)

In 1956, when St. Luke's Free Episcopal Church in Phillipsburg marked its 100th anniversary, this illustration of its new sanctuary, completed just the year before, graced the cover of the service bulletin. The procession hymn that day seemed fitting: "O God, our help in ages past, Our hope for years to come, Our shelter from the stormy blast, And our eternal home." (Courtesy of the Episcopal Diocese of Newark.)

St. Mary's in Sparta was founded as a mission of St. Peter's in Morristown in 1919, when the Sussex County community was a rural hamlet. Its five parishioners worshipped in a sanctuary on Main Street, above, where six frame structures served the church. By 1958, the building of a new $175,000 church on Conestoga Trail was announced in the *Newark Evening News*. "None of the present buildings are of permanent construction," said Rev. Harold Shaffer, vicar. The architect of the new 300-seat church was Robert L. Clothier of Newton. By St. Mary's 50th anniversary in 1969, there was still some unfinished business: the parish remained a mission. "Some of our parishioners may not understand quite fully what this means," said a church flier on a capital campaign. "It means that as affluent as our parish is, its stewardship to the church is that poor . . . Does this possibility not give enough cause for anyone to wonder and do some honest 'soul-searching'?" (Courtesy of the Episcopal Diocese of Newark.)

Tracing its beginnings to June 29, 1881, St. Peter's Episcopal Church in Washington would later lay claim to conducting a host of parties for fund-raising and fellowship. A St. Valentine Party in 1947 unleashed donations of lumber and other material to lay a new floor, paint the interior, and purchase cassocks, cottas, and a red carpet for the center aisle. At that point, St. James' Episcopal Church in Montclair donated a new pulpit to the parish. That year, a Couple's Club was formed, which by 1951 was known as the Nut Club. Each month, a couple would come prepared with some game, whether it be a "hot doggies roast" at Eagle's Nest Farm or a Halloween dance. "We admit that all this sounds too ridiculous for a church activity," read a parish publication of the day, "however, we feel that there is plenty of room for real-life expression in the realm of humor and fun." (Courtesy of the Episcopal Diocese of Newark.)

It has been a centerpiece of Hackettstown since 1859. St. James' Episcopal Church was established on a half-acre corner lot in the center of downtown and is one of the town's oldest structures. But it was not an easy start. That year a violent tornado swept through town, according to the *Hackettstown Gazette* of July 8. "In the twinkling of an eye, the skill and industry of the master builders and the labors of the workmen were prostrated at one fell swoop! The entire structure was lifted as by a whirlwind, the whole pile falling directly upon the foundations," read the newspaper account. "The work, however, will soon be commenced and prosecuted with vigor until completion." (Courtesy of the Episcopal Diocese of Newark.)

Christ Church, Newton, can trace its origin to December 29, 1769, when a "Congregation in Communion with the Church of England" was organized in what was then called New Town. The parish had been incorporated by royal charter on August 15, 1774. Today that sheepskin charter hangs under glass on the west wall of the nave. In 1911, above, the writer of this postcard penned, "We attended here and were married in this church."

Six

SPREADING THE WORD

He is risen, he is risen! Tell it out with joyful voice:
he has burst his three days' prison;
let the whole wide earth rejoice; death is conquered,
we are free, Christ has won the victory.

—Hymn No. 180, *The Hymnal* 1982

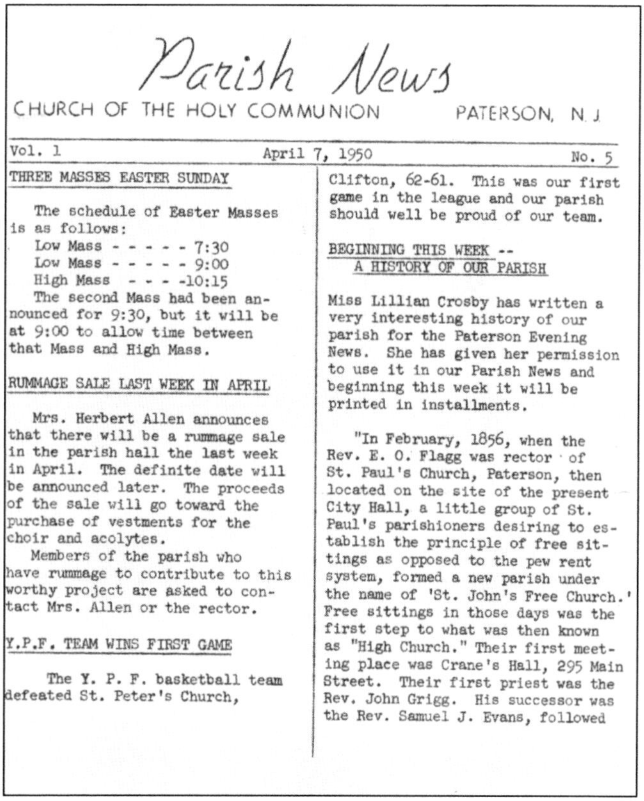

Parish News

CHURCH OF THE HOLY COMMUNION PATERSON, N. J.

Vol. 1 April 7, 1950 No. 5

THREE MASSES EASTER SUNDAY

The schedule of Easter Masses is as follows:
Low Mass - - - - - 7:30
Low Mass - - - - - 9:00
High Mass - - - -10:15
The second Mass had been announced for 9:30, but it will be at 9:00 to allow time between that Mass and High Mass.

RUMMAGE SALE LAST WEEK IN APRIL

Mrs. Herbert Allen announces that there will be a rummage sale in the parish hall the last week in April. The definite date will be announced later. The proceeds of the sale will go toward the purchase of vestments for the choir and acolytes.
Members of the parish who have rummage to contribute to this worthy project are asked to contact Mrs. Allen or the rector.

Y.P.F. TEAM WINS FIRST GAME

The Y. P. F. basketball team defeated St. Peter's Church, Clifton, 62-61. This was our first game in the league and our parish should well be proud of our team.

BEGINNING THIS WEEK --
A HISTORY OF OUR PARISH

Miss Lillian Crosby has written a very interesting history of our parish for the Paterson Evening News. She has given her permission to use it in our Parish News and beginning this week it will be printed in installments.

"In February, 1856, when the Rev. E. O. Flagg was rector of St. Paul's Church, Paterson, then located on the site of the present City Hall, a little group of St. Paul's parishioners desiring to establish the principle of free sittings as opposed to the pew rent system, formed a new parish under the name of 'St. John's Free Church.' Free sittings in those days was the first step to what was then known as "High Church." Their first meeting place was Crane's Hall, 295 Main Street. Their first priest was the Rev. John Grigg. His successor was the Rev. Samuel J. Evans, followed

In 1950, the newsletter of the Church of the Holy Communion in Paterson was packed with history and was a snapshot of commerce in the "Silk City." The cornerstone was laid on May 20, 1871, at a church constructed at Carroll and Pearl Streets. The blue trap rock for the church was donated by John Ryle, a former mayor and Paterson's pioneer silk manufacturer. (Courtesy of the Episcopal Diocese of Newark.)

ST·PETER'S·RECORD

MORRISTOWN·NEW·JERSEY

VOLUME XVII JUNE, 1925 No. 3

WESTERN COUNTIES MISSION

The Rector's Statement

The DIOCESE OF NEWARK is made up of the seven most northerly counties of New Jersey, together with the township of Summit. Morristown is almost exactly half way across it, from east to west.

East of us are the cities—Newark, Paterson, Jersey City and the like, and fast-growing suburban towns.

West of us, Dover, Newton and Phillipsburg are the only communities of any considerable size. It is a region made up of small towns, separated by wide rural spaces.

Warren and Sussex Counties are almost entirely rural.

The Episcopal Church has a ministry for dwellers in the country as much as for those in the city. This is not always recognized. The rural work often is given second place. But in a growing number of dioceses, of which ours is one, efforts are being made to do what cries out to be done in the country.

It is not done easily. People in the remote country places have their own problems and habits and ideas. Men and women of rare sanity, as well as of rare consecration of life, are needed for any efforts that the Church is to make in this connection.

THE REV. EDWIN S. FORD
Western Counties Missionary

From the start, the WESTERN COUNTIES MISSION has been singularly fortunate as to this. No priest of the Church is better suited to his special post than is the Reverend Edwin S. Ford, whom five years ago this parish sent into Warren and Sussex Counties with a roving commission to do what he could in a huge, untouched rural field. It was a commission to search out all people in need of any sort, whether or not having any Church connection, and to minister to them as his judgment might dictate.

A year or so ago, he was given a co-worker in the person of Miss Mary Louise Rowland. Here also the Mission was singularly favored. Miss Rowland has spoken in our Parish House, under the auspices of the St. Peter's Diocesan Guild, and those who heard her would endorse the highest statements in her praise. Although not technically a deaconess, she took the training as such, and went directly from it to help in the Western Counties.

The part of ST. PETER'S CHURCH in this Mission has been to have immense pride in its success, sympathy with the difficulties of the devoted young missionaries, eager interest in the details of what they are doing, and a willing readiness to provide what

The June 1925 edition of *St. Peter's Record* carried word of the work in the Western Counties Mission by Rev. Edwin S. Ford, who was dispatched by the Morristown church to the rural outpost as a missionary. "Men and woman of rare sanity, as well as of rare consecration of life, are needed," the rector said. (Courtesy of the Episcopal Diocese of Newark.)

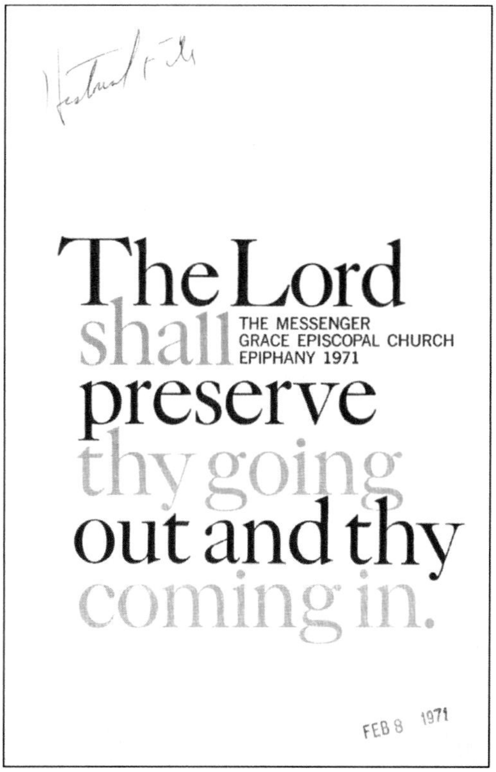

In the realm of communication, the parish handbook was a virtual who's who. At Grace Episcopal Church in Madison back in 1958, the 20-page handbook had the telephone numbers of officers of the many guilds, including the men's club and the Young People's Fellowship (YPF). It even listed the 42 young people who were away at school and colleges. "Seek to keep in touch with them," the handbook said. The news extended to the *Messenger*, the parish newsletter. In the 1971 edition, readers spotted the headline, "Thou Shall Not Lie!" over a story on 67 male parishioners trying out a lie-detector device as they "squirmed in their seats." (Courtesy of the Episcopal Diocese of Newark.)

St. Matthew's Weekly

Vol. IV. SEPTEMBER 19, 1920 No. 221

ST. MATTHEW'S WEEKLY

Sixteenth Sunday after Trinity, 1920

This paper is published every Sunday by the Rector, Wardens and Vestry of St. Matthew's Church, Jersey City.

Editor—The Rector, 266 Armstrong Avenue

Business Manager—Miss Ada Aspinwall, 119 Bostwick Avenue.

Checks should be made payable to St. Matthew's Church, and sent to Miss Aspinwall.

Communications—All Communications should be in the Editor's hands by Thursday noon. The Editor cannot accept verbal communications.

Office Hours—The Rector may be seen in the vestry any day, except Sunday and Monday from 1 to 2 o'clock.

UNITED THANK OFFERING

Mrs. Leasondale asks that all who have the blue boxes for the United Thank Offering for Missions will please bring them in by Sunday evening, September 26th.

BARN DANCE

The Esther Guild will give a Barn Dance Monday evening, September 27th, at 8 o'clock. Gentlemen's tickets 35 cents; ladies' 25 cents. Prizes will be awarded for the best costumes.

A MISSION

A most important event will take place in St. Matthew's Church in the week of October 3, and all readers of the Weekly are urged to take note, remember, and disseminate what information they can among their friends.

On Sunday evening, October 3rd, there will begin an eight day mission conducted by Archdeacon Webber of the Diocese of Florida, a missioner of great ability, and whose work is well known throughout the American Church. For many years Archdeacon Webber has given himself entirely to this kind of work having no parochial charge whatever, and in consequence is a specialist in preaching missions. The Rector has known Archdeacon Wbeber for nine or ten years and has had experience of his missions. He is in considerable demand all over the country and is already booked for several weeks ahead. He has lately returned from far off India, where he conducted successful missions at various posts of the Anglican Church in that country.

Archdeacon Webber will be present at the morning service of Oct. 3, when the service will take the nature of a preparation for the mission; but the mission proper will begin in the evening of that day, continuing throughout the week—every evening at 8 o'clock—and end with the evening service on Sunday October 10; a special service for women being held on Saturday afternoon, October 9th, and for men on Sunday afternoon, October 10th, at 4 o'clock.

St. Matthew's Episcopal Church

Fulton Avenue and Boulevard, Jersey City, New Jersey

The *Weekly*, as it was called on September 19, 1920, let parishioners of St. Matthew's Episcopal Church in Jersey City keep abreast of such things as the "Barn Dance," with prizes for best costumes, and the arrival of a missioner who was to tell of his Anglican endeavors in faraway India. (Courtesy of the Episcopal Diocese of Newark.)

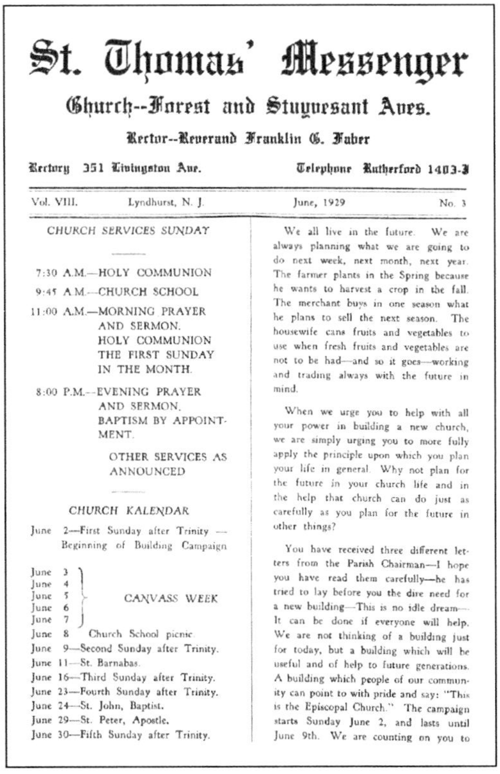

St. Thomas' Messenger

Church--Forest and Stuyvesant Aves.

Rector--Reverend Franklin G. Faber

Rectory 351 Livingston Ave. Telephone Rutherford 1403-J

Vol. VIII. Lyndhurst, N. J. June, 1929 No. 3

CHURCH SERVICES SUNDAY

7:30 A.M.—HOLY COMMUNION

9:45 A.M.—CHURCH SCHOOL

11:00 A.M.—MORNING PRAYER AND SERMON. HOLY COMMUNION THE FIRST SUNDAY IN THE MONTH.

8:00 P.M.—EVENING PRAYER AND SERMON. BAPTISM BY APPOINTMENT.

OTHER SERVICES AS ANNOUNCED

CHURCH KALENDAR

June 2—First Sunday after Trinity — Beginning of Building Campaign

June 3, June 4, June 5, June 6, June 7 — CANVASS WEEK

June 8 Church School picnic.

June 9—Second Sunday after Trinity.

June 11—St. Barnabas.

June 16—Third Sunday after Trinity.

June 23—Fourth Sunday after Trinity.

June 24—St. John, Baptist.

June 29—St. Peter, Apostle.

June 30—Fifth Sunday after Trinity.

We all live in the future. We are always planning what we are going to do next week, next month, next year. The farmer plants in the Spring because he wants to harvest a crop in the fall. The merchant buys in one season what he plans to sell the next season. The housewife cans fruits and vegetables to use when fresh fruits and vegetables are not to be had—and so it goes—working and trading always with the future in mind.

When we urge you to help with all your power in building a new church, we are simply urging you to more fully apply the principle upon which you plan your life in general. Why not plan for the future in your church life and in the help that church can do just as carefully as you plan for the future in other things?

You have received three different letters from the Parish Chairman—I hope you have read them carefully—he has tried to lay before you the dire need for a new building—This is no idle dream—It can be done if everyone will help. We are not thinking of a building just for today, but a building which will be useful and of help to future generations. A building which people of our community can point to with pride and say: "This is the Episcopal Church." The campaign starts Sunday June 2, and lasts until June 9th. We are counting on you to

St. Thomas' Messenger in June 1929 carried some welcome summer news for the Lyndhurst parish: "The Annual Church School Bus Ride and Picnic." The destination was a New Jersey landmark, Bertrand Island at Lake Hopatcong, with 30 acres of prime picnic grounds. There for some 70 years until 1983, an amusement park was a big draw for thrill seekers. (Courtesy of the Episcopal Diocese of Newark.)

In Montclair, the booklet *St. Luke's, More Beautiful* offers some insights into the life of the early parish. One rector, Rev. F. B. Carter, was said to have disapproved of church fairs, simply because too many people wanted to run them. "He retired in 1912," the article reports, "after at least one earlier attempt when he told his wife he was going to turn in his resignation, and she told him he was not." In a 1949 magazine article, the parish was dubbed "Montclair's Incomparable St. Luke's," with the subhead, "One of the truly intellectual churches of the nation seeks answers to questions that seem to have no answers." (Courtesy of the Episcopal Diocese of Newark.)

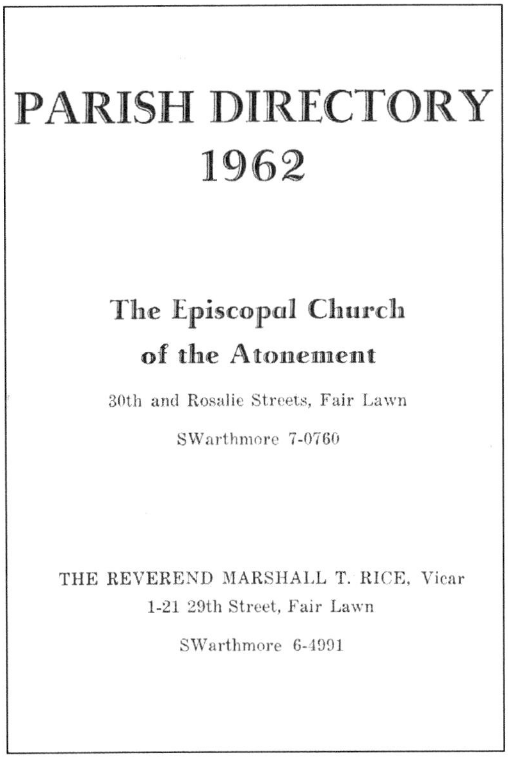
PARISH DIRECTORY
1962

The Episcopal Church
of the Atonement

30th and Rosalie Streets, Fair Lawn

SWarthmore 7-0760

THE REVEREND MARSHALL T. RICE, Vicar
1-21 29th Street, Fair Lawn

SWarthmore 6-4991

Some 24 pages of advertising were sold for the 1962 parish directory of the Episcopal Church of the Atonement in Fair Lawn, then led by Rev. Marshall T. Rice, vicar. Among the many advertisers was Radburn Paint and Wallpaper Company. The planned community of Radburn, begun in 1929 but never finished, was billed as the first "Town for the Motor Age." The neighborhood is listed on both the New Jersey and National Register of Historic Places. (Courtesy of the Episcopal Diocese of Newark.)

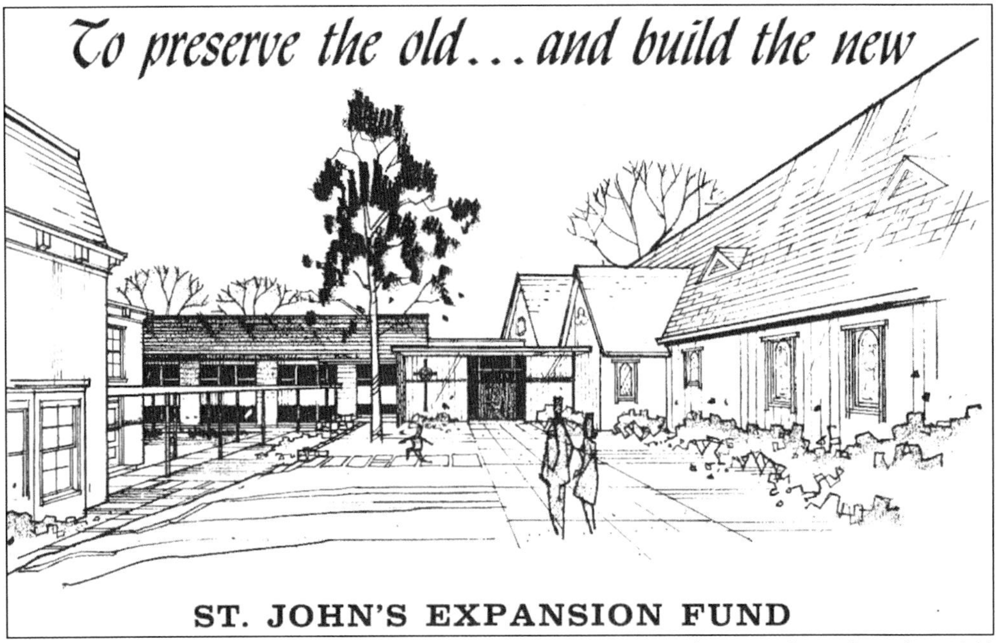

There was nothing like an expansion campaign to excite a parish, as evidenced in this 1960 pitch for St. John's Episcopal Church in Boonton. "So often the general day-in and day-out routine of parish life can begin to seem dull," wrote Rev. Paul C. Deckenbach. "But now you and I have been called upon by the very pressure of circumstances—the demands of growth—to go the extra mile for God." (Courtesy of the Episcopal Diocese of Newark.)

SAINT ANDREW'S PARISH RECORD

SOUTH ORANGE, NEW JERSEY

Published Weekly

Vol. XV **NOVEMBER 23, 1924** **No. 2**

Rector: REV. F. CRESWICK TODD, 359 Hartford Road, South Orange

Rector's Secretary, GERTRUDE D. HITCH, 156 Irving Ave., South Orange
(Office Hours—Mornings except Saturdays)

Organist and Choirmaster, VERNON EVILLE, 9 East 17th St., N. Y.
Acting Organist, MISS MILDRED TILL, 101 Park St., East Orange

Treasurer, W. H. LAKE, 606 Berkeley Ave., Orange

Chairman Envelope Committee, W. S. SKEATS, 743 Scotland Road, Orange

SERVICES

(All Seats Free)

Holy Communion: All Sundays, 8 A. M. First Sundays and Greater Festivals, 11 A. M. Holy Days within the week (when announced), 10 A. M.

Holy Baptism: Second, fourth and fifth Sundays, 12.30 P. M., and by appointment.

Morning Prayer and Sermon: (except first Sundays), 11 A. M.

The Church Sunday School: 9.45–10.55 A. M.

MEETINGS

Young People's Society	Sundays	7.40 p. m.
The Men of St. Andrew's	Second Mondays	8.30 p. m.
Girls Friendly Society	First Mondays	7 p. m.
Girls Friendly Society	Other Mondays	7.30 p. m.
Woman's Guild and Auxiliary	Tuesdays	10 a. m.-5. p. m.
Boy Choir	Tuesdays	4 p. m.
Boy Choir	Thursdays	7.30 p. m.
Senior Choir Club	First Thursdays	9 p. m.
Girl Scouts	Wednesdays	3.30 p. m.
Mothers' Meeting	Thursdays	2.30 p. m.
Boy Scouts	Fridays	7.45 p. m.
Junior Scouts	Fridays	7.45 p. m.
Altar and Font Guild		at the call of the Directress

The year 1924 apparently was not a bad one for St. Andrew's Episcopal Church in South Orange. "A Wonderful Year" proclaimed a headline inside the pages of the weekly *Parish Record*. "Last year the rector rubbed his eyes and wondered if he were awake to see that we had 225 members on our Sunday School lists," the writer said. "Last Sunday we all rubbed our eyes and ears too, when we found that the attendance was 226 or eleven more than we ever had." (Courtesy of the Episcopal Diocese of Newark.)

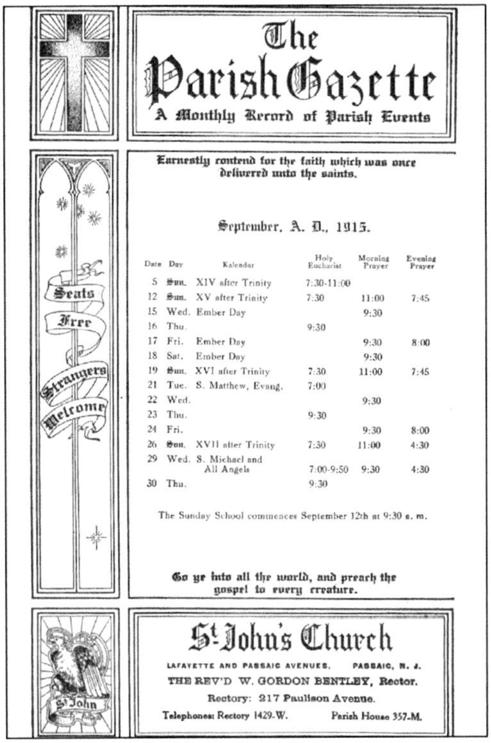

The Parish Gazette

A Monthly Record of Parish Events

Earnestly contend for the faith which was once delivered unto the saints.

Seats Free

Strangers Welcome

September, A. D., 1915.

Date	Day	Kalendar	Holy Eucharist	Morning Prayer	Evening Prayer
5	Sun.	XIV after Trinity	7:30-11:00		
12	Sun.	XV after Trinity	7:30	11:00	7:45
15	Wed.	Ember Day		9:30	
16	Thu.		9:30		
17	Fri.	Ember Day		9:30	8:00
18	Sat.	Ember Day		9:30	
19	Sun.	XVI after Trinity	7:30	11:00	7:45
21	Tue.	S. Matthew, Evang.	7:00		
22	Wed.			9:30	
23	Thu.		9:30		
24	Fri.			9:30	8:00
26	Sun.	XVII after Trinity	7:30	11:00	4:30
29	Wed.	S. Michael and All Angels	7:00-9:50	9:30	4:30
30	Thu.		9:30		

The Sunday School commences September 12th at 9:30 a. m.

Go ye into all the world, and preach the gospel to every creature.

St. John's Church

LAFAYETTE AND PASSAIC AVENUES, PASSAIC, N. J.

THE REV'D W. GORDON BENTLEY, Rector.

Rectory: 217 Paulison Avenue.

Telephones: Rectory 1429-W. Parish House 357-M.

St. John

Inside the *Parish Gazette* of St. John's Episcopal Church in Passaic, Rev. W. Gordon Bentley, rector, in 1915 prodded would-be teachers to join Sunday school. "The Sunday School teaching force needs recruits, as some of the former faithful teachers are obliged to drop out," he wrote. "Please see to it that the children that you have solemnly promised to have taught . . . are sent to the Church School on the first Sunday of its session, that they come in time, and that they come regularly." (Courtesy of the Episcopal Diocese of Newark.)

THE *Messenger*

SAINT PETER'S EPISCOPAL CHURCH
Roseland Avenue, Essex Fells, N.J. 07021

Vol. 30 No. 10 June 1969

WORD FROM LIBERIA

The Rector received the following letter of thanks from the Rt. Rev. Dillard H. Brown, Bishop of Liberia our companion diocese in West Africa.

Bishop Brown

Dear Mr. Whitley,

We are most grateful for the generous cheque of $514.20 from the Church School at St. Peter's. I am deeply impressed by this most needed contribution. Please express to the Church

WELL-DESERVED RECOGNITION

The Fall-Spring term of the Church School will close on Sunday, June 15th. Special sessions are being planned for each grade by the teachers. On Sunday, June 22nd at the 10 o' clock service, all of the teaching staff will be recognized by the Rector. It is our hope that all parents and members of the Church School will make a special effort to attend this service and join the Clergy, and the Christian Education Department in showing their deepest appreciation and thanks to the staff for their faithful service all year. They are:

9 A.M. Session - Edwin Fox, Dean; Evelyn Loinaz,

The pages of the *Messenger* of St. Peter's, Essex Fells, in 1969, carried an "Unclassified Ad" with the picture of Vee Hodson at the receptionist desk and a call for volunteers. "The job primarily involves answering the phone from 9:00 a.m. until noon and from 1 until 4 p.m., the greeting of people who come to the office on business, and, on occasion, helping with odd jobs around the office," she wrote. (Courtesy of the Episcopal Diocese of Newark.)

Seven

UNDER GOD'S GREAT SKY

Morning has broken like the first morning,
blackbird has spoken like the first bird,
Praise for the singing! Praise for the morning!
Praise for them springing fresh from the Word!

—Hymn No. 8, *The Hymnal* 1982

The season three, 1991, version of Eagle's Nest Camp gathers for a group portrait. It was just eight years until the coming merger with the Lutherans' Camp Beisler. (Courtesy of the Episcopal Diocese of Newark.)

The flag raising was a morning rite at Eagle's Nest Camp, as it was at most American summer camps. In its early days, the camp also encompassed the Girls' Friendly Society's Holiday House, where a young people's conference in 1929 sparked this account by M. Estelle Burrill, which was published in the *Newark Churchman*. "Four girls sat together under a big tree and their thoughts

all turned to the Younger Members' Conference. 'Didn't you have the best time in your life?' said Jane. 'That house was so 'comfy' with its large living room; and what meals! Haven't I gained five pounds?'" (Courtesy of the Episcopal Diocese of Newark.)

Visitors were allowed only on Saturdays at Eagle's Nest Farm in the early days. In 1929, just seven years after its founding, campers had healthy appetites, according to an article in the *Newark Churchman*. In that "contest," however, the boys edged out the girls, 12,952 meals to 11,750. (Courtesy of the Episcopal Diocese of Newark.)

Eagle's Nest Camp's 180 acres provided plenty of room to frolic, as campers do in this undated photograph. In May 1949, the camp was also put to use for conferences, with topics that included "The Prayer Book in Action" and "The Practical Application of the Holy Communion." (Courtesy of the Episcopal Diocese of Newark.)

At Eagle's Nest Farm Camp in 1922, two years after its founding, this group posed outside a cabin. The people are identified as, from left to right, Mrs. L., Mae Webster, Sue Young, Sally Chastiney, Jack Travis, Bill Lockon, Helen Sterling, and Oliver. (Courtesy of the Episcopal Diocese of Newark.)

Girls dart across the field in this updated picture from the old Eagle's Nest Camp, which in a historic 1999 merger joined with Camp Beisler, operated by the Lutherans, and formed what today is known as Cross Roads. The union created the first and only camp in America operated jointly by separate denominations. (Courtesy of the Episcopal Diocese of Newark.)

Many of the girls at Eagle's Nest Camp, in addition to taking up archery and other sports, also belonged to the GFS. It was a busy group. In 1949, for instance, they raised money for the National GFS Mission, namely the support of an English teacher in Western China. "Last year our motto was 'Gung Ho,' or 'it can be done'; this year our motto is 'Moy Do' or 'Do it again,'" read an account in the *Newark Churchman*. (Courtesy of the Episcopal Diocese of Newark.)

In the 1960s, campers enjoyed the lake. When out of the water, they read the camp newsletter, the *Egg*, whose pages carried stories written by campers. One authored by Kathy Smith told a tale about counselor Rusty Garthwaite of Montclair. "This is Rusty's second year as a counselor at E.N.C., and his most embarrassing moment here was when he fell out of his canoe in front of his whole canoe class." (Courtesy of the Episcopal Diocese of Newark, photograph by George H. Rackett Jr. of East Orange.)

It paid to advertise in the *Newark Churchman*, the diocesan publication. In February 1957, when this advertisement ran, Eagle's Nest Camp was enlisting most campers for $30 a week. (Courtesy of the Episcopal Diocese of Newark.)

Eagle's Nest Camp
STAFF 1977

For an inside look at the summer session of 1977, above, there were plentiful stories from campers and counselors alike in the newsletter, the *Egg*, which during the hot July session that year was renamed the *Fried Egg*. It included riddles, such as this one attributed to Ben and John Korinski: "Q. Why is a barn noisy? A. The cows have horns." And it included heartfelt farewells, such as this one by a girl named Sue: "As we leave Eagle's Nest Camp, God is with us . . . Because of the spirit we have shared, each of us is somehow changed. We may go back to the same old places and do the same old things, but we can never be exactly the same as we were two weeks ago. I pray that each of us will take the spirit of love known here and grow in it." (Courtesy of the Episcopal Diocese of Newark.)

The 1980 session at Eagle's Nest Camp, like any other, had its own uniqueness, as outlined in the camp newsletter. "What would happen at E.N.C, IF . . . Phyllis wasn't a priest? Gordon T. didn't have a song to teach? Mike didn't have long hair? Kathy H. didn't have a whistle . . . Scott had three more weeks of camp? . . . Debbie didn't have sneakers that glow?" (Courtesy of the Episcopal Diocese of Newark.)

The Church of the Messiah in Chester was the scene of his "holdover camp" in 1990, a place where campers staying for multiple sessions could "hold over" for the weekend rather than go home. The vicar, Joe Pickard, is just below the *T* of *The Messiah* on the sign. That year, Kathryn King, far right, was diocesan camp director. "We would arrive in mass, sing at some point, and generally try to promote good will about the camp," said King, now the rector of All Saints Episcopal Church in Bergenfield. "The visit to Messiah was timed to coordinate with . . . The Amazing—only seen in Chester—Turtle Races!" (Courtesy of the Episcopal Diocese of Newark.)

It was a rite of summer at Eagle's Nest Camp in Delaware, New Jersey: the staff photograph. In 1969, the staffers are identified as, from left to right, (first row) Fred Yoto, Chip Thomas, Doug Hargrove, Mona Lomyn Nadella, Leah Jackson, Lee S'nail, David S'nail, Roberta Youmans, John Zeevalk, Buzzy Nesley, Gordy Re, Denny Gunn, and Bill Kelly; (second row) John Tomlinson, Elaine Robertson, Jackie Eck, Laurie Richardson, Jeri Sardella, Morton Dow, Grethchen Hogeboom, Wanda Moyse, Robin Smith, Linda Townsend, Pat Dillon, Norma Margrove, Janet Dahl, Dot Youmans, Leena Lindstrom, Jane Mullins, and Robert Godthaas; (third row) Wayne Murray, Dave Tucker, Peter Chad, Mike Peck, Rick Whritenour, Ken Hillas, Ed White, Dave Lewen, Simho Vinno, Father King, Barry Ahrenot, Terry Gunn, Rusty Garthwaite, and Mark Decker. (Courtesy of the Episcopal Diocese of Newark.)

Eagle's Nest Camp's 50th anniversary was in 1972, the year these session II juniors gathered for this camp picture. In a farewell message that season, "Whitey" summed it up this way: "It isn't always easy to live together as closely as we must in a camping situation. Sometimes it must have seemed pretty hard to try to understand our cabin-mates—to smile, and give that last ounce of Christian love. At Eagle's Nest, we call that 'going the extra mile.' Remember the good. Forgive the bad." (Courtesy of the Episcopal Diocese of Newark.)